Third Child:
Blurred Identity

BlurredIdentity23@gmail.com

Some names and locations have been changed or omitted to protect the privacy of certain individuals.

ISBN: 978-0-578-94179-0

1. Colorism 2. Sibling Rivalry 3. Racism 4. Jim Crow
5. Interracial Relationships 6. African American Woman
7. Sexual Assault

Printed in the United States of America

To Edwin & Neffe,
Best Wishes. Enjoy!

Patricia Sizer

12/4/2021

Third Child:
Blurred Identity

Challenges within the Family, Race, and Society

A MEMOIR

PATRICIA SIZER

Contents

Preface................................... vii

Early Years 1

Ancestry...................................11

Grandpa Sizer 25

Surviving.................................45

St. John Elementary School................61

Balty Elementary School 71

Miss Upton...............................81

Sizer's Place.............................91

Aunt Eunice 111

Bad News...............................123

Union High School.......................129

A New Addition to Our Family 139

A Special Opportunity....................145

Transitioning to College..................151

College Life 157

Beginning My Career 171

A Night of Terror 179

An Early Death 187

Bobby 195

Reflections 205

Acknowledgments 211

Notes...................................213

Bibliography 215

Preface

When I began writing this memoir many years ago, I was single and a few years into the retirement phase of my life. There were periods when I did not write at all, and sometimes I only wrote during the summer. Life happened. At first, I intended to write about me as the third child in my family and the challenges associated with it. But as I began writing, I realized that there were other things that had impacted my life even more. So I began with my earliest memory and ended in the early 1970s because these years were more impressionable and formative. Certain events have stayed with me and, in some cases, haunted me for years. Some degree of discrimination seemed to have existed in the three major aspects of my life: family and race, which I had no control over, and society.

I have written about events that I remember from my perspective. While describing some of them, names have deliberately been omitted or changed because it is possible that these individuals were not impacted the same way as I and might not remember or may even deny that these things ever happened or happened in the way that I have described. I have attempted to use the terms Colored, Negro, Black, and African American within the context of the time; however, in some instances these terms have been used interchangeably. I am grateful for having the opportunity to share my experiences and the impact they have had on me. Part of the title of the book, *Blurred Identity*, implies confusion and lack of clarity, but as life has progressed, the reasons for some of these occurrences have become clearer and have been accepted as a part of my unchangeable past.

Early Years

One of my earliest memories is that of leaning over a beautiful, old, wooden banister watching my grandfather, my father's father, raise the netting from my grandmother's face and kiss her. I have seen pictures of myself at a younger age than I was at that time, yet I have no recollection of those times. However, this image has remained with me. The year was 1950, and I was a little over four years old. Perhaps it was one of the many things I witnessed during my lifetime that left a lasting impression, one that influenced the way I would later view love.

This banister had always been a place for having fun. I would slide down it every chance I got, against the wishes of my grandparents, of course. After a long, fast, smooth slide down, I would have to grip it very tightly so that I wouldn't slide all the way off and end up face-down on the floor. But this time it was different. My grandfather was kissing my grandmother for the last time. The netting was covering her as she lay in repose in the living room of their home. I remember that the casket had a white, satin lining and a sheer fabric, much like that of a veil, hung from the opened top of the casket to its bottom edge. Grandpa raised the netting, leaned into the casket, and kissed Grandma good-bye. They had indeed kept their vows, "Until death do us part." I felt frightened and sad for him all at the same time. Of course, I didn't completely understand death. This was the first wake that I had witnessed and the first dead person I had ever seen.

Back in those days, it was a common practice to have the wakes of family members take place at home. Even in the 1970s, people in the rural areas, especially in the neighborhood where I lived, had friends, neighbors, and church members view the bodies of loved ones in the home of the deceased. In 1971, my mother's casket was placed in the living room of our home. As she lay in repose, there was a brief time during the day when no one was in the living room except me, so I decided to say good-bye to her. I examined everything that had been done to present my mom in the manner that she would have wanted. Days before the wake, the mortician had asked for some of her undergarments and lipstick. This was unexpected, but we complied. Her hair had been styled just as we had requested, the red lipstick had been applied, and her fingernails had been manicured. She was always particular about her fingernails; she kept them at a medium length with bright-colored polish. I noticed her hands that I had held the day she died were still discolored as a result of poor circulation. As apprehensive as I was, I found the courage to touch one of them. Her hand was as cold as ice. The dining room was two steps up from the living room. I had to sleep in the bedroom on the other side of the dining room during that time. The casket was visible from there, and it was extremely difficult being so near my mother's lifeless body. It was really an eerie feeling.

4

Our community was called Chilesburg. It was a small, rural neighborhood in Caroline County, Virginia. Our family homes were a little less than one hundred yards apart and consisted of my paternal aunts, uncles, cousins, and grandparents. There were six houses within yelling distance of each other. In one of those houses was a lady that I did not discover was my aunt until I was in college. Later, five more houses were constructed for my older brother, my first cousins, and another aunt, all on my father's side of the family.

One of my father's uncles, who drank a lot, built my father's and his two brothers' homes using the same floor plan; from the outside, they all looked alike. But several years later, Dad and Mom added a living room with a fireplace on one side of the house and a screened porch on the other side of the house. The living room was as large as two rooms combined. With the exception of the entrance door, there were windows on the entire front of the living room. A funny thing happened one day when I was about five years old. I was standing beside my mother near the kitchen stove while my great-uncle was working in the bedroom upstairs. All of a sudden, I heard this cracking sound and a loud thump; he had fallen through the floor into the dining room! I assumed he had been drinking and missed a step while trying to maneuver on the unfinished floor. Fortunately, he was not seriously injured.

We had indoor plumbing in the kitchen, but at that time, we did not have a bathroom with indoor plumbing. Even though my father could not afford to install the necessary plumbing, our great-uncle built a room to accommodate a bathroom on the first floor for future use. The bathroom was located downstairs off the hallway near the staircase, between the kitchen and Mom and Dad's bedroom. Since my brothers, sister, and I slept in the bedrooms upstairs, within a few steps of the stairs, we could walk straight into the bathroom. This made it convenient for everyone. Within a couple of years, the bathroom interior was completed and fully furnished with all of the necessary items and fixtures. Until then, like most of the homes in the neighborhood, we had an outhouse.

We didn't have a farm as such. But we had a chicken coop, not too far from the outhouse, where we'd gather fresh eggs and fresh chickens for meals. We also had a pigpen. When the hogs were killed, it was an event that my father and his brothers shared—not only the butchering but the meat was shared as well. The women of the three neighboring Sizer families processed the sausage, chitterlings, pork loin, etc. What wasn't eaten while the meat was fresh, was smoked or frozen. We always had small gardens in the spring and summer. I helped plant some of the vegetables and later helped harvest them. After gathering vegetables from the garden, we would sit under a shady tree in our backyard and shell lima beans, shuck corn, and snap string beans. What we didn't eat fresh from the garden, Mom would can or freeze to supplement our meals during the winter months.

My paternal grandfather, Arthur J. Sizer, had acres of land that he inherited. He sold my daddy, Frank Chester Sizer, a portion of land so he could build his home. Daddy was the youngest boy and the twelfth of 13 children. When his brothers returned home from World War II and decided to build their homes, they purchased land from my dad. All three houses were on the same side of the road, spaced equal distance apart. My aunt who lived on the opposite side of the road, the same side as Grandpa, purchased her home from my grandfather's brother. I was told that this was the original homeplace—a log cabin where my great-grandfather (John Karr Sizer) and my great-grandmother (Hawzie Coleman) lived. When I was growing up, the house they lived in was known as Aunt Ruth's house. The house still had logs in the ceiling from the original cabin where my great-grandparents lived during the middle-to-late 1800s. However, over the years we were told that there was another house behind this house where John Karr Sizer also lived. I guess this was to avoid authorities questioning a White man and Black woman living together.

"Cousin Carrie" (we always called her this, not knowing until later in life that she was our aunt) lived in a house on the same side of the road as ours, directly across from the old homeplace. Her home was approximately a quarter of a mile to the east of ours. During her adult life, she spent some years in New York. Cousin Carrie eventually moved back home to Chilesburg, where she lived with her mother, Lucy Baber. (I am not sure how Miss Lucy acquired her property; however, my sister said that Miss Lucy purchased it.) Miss Lucy's brother was a minister, and we called him Work Baber. He lived about a mile or two down the road, west of our home. He and my grandfather were friends. It seemed strange that Miss Lucy was the only one with a home in our neighborhood who was not related to us. I don't know if Grandpa gave her this property because he fathered a child with her or if Work Baber actually owned it. Also, the Baber family's cemetery was obtrusively located between our home and my uncle's home.

One of my most treasured memories of living in this close community is Christmas morning. Of course, prior to this special day, we had to find a Christmas tree. Hunting for a tree was always fun and challenging. In the forest behind our home there were over 15 acres of land owned by my dad, so we had the freedom to search for just the right one. I don't recall that anyone in the neighborhood ever bought a tree. My family's favorite was the cedar tree. When we thought we had the perfect one, we would drag it back to the house. There were a few times when the tree was much larger than expected, and cutting the base still wasn't enough for it to fit into our living room, so we would have to go back into the forest to find another one. The aroma of the cedar tree permeated the house, which has created a lasting sensory memory of Christmas for me. We used decorations just the same as today, with the exception of angel hair and icicles. Angel hair was very fine, made from spun glass, and would cut like glass—we handled it with our bare hands, which was not a good idea. I distinctly recall the beautiful glow of the lights when we placed angel hair over them. Icicles were usually silver, about a quarter of an inch wide, thinner than a sheet of paper, and maybe 18 or 20 inches long. We would hang them on the outer edges of the tree limbs. You seldom see these anymore.

Before my brothers, Frank Jr. (Bootsie) and Ronald (Ronnie); my sister, Clara Lucille (Lucille); and I went to bed on Christmas Eve, we always left Santa cookies and milk on the kitchen table. Lucille was the oldest child, next was Bootsie, and then me. There were approximately two years between each of the first three of us, but almost six years between Ronnie and me. On Christmas morning we would wake up early to see what Santa had left under the tree. Of course, we would wake up a few times, usually too early, before our parents would allow us to come downstairs. Although the time came when Lucille, Bootsie, and I no longer believed in Santa Claus, we still had to wait because of our baby brother, Ronnie. One Christmas, Santa left tiny switches and ashes in a cast-iron frying pan on the kitchen stove to let us know that we hadn't been so good that year. I don't know where my parents got that idea from; I have never heard of anyone else doing this. We did get some presents that Christmas, but not as many as before.

Before we went door-to-door to collect our presents from our paternal grandparents, aunts, and uncles, the family tradition on Christmas morning was to have a quick breakfast that consisted of oyster stew and saltine crackers. When we arrived at Grandpa Sizer's home, he would actually have real white socks hanging from the fireplace mantel in the living room for each of us with a tangerine or orange, raisins still on the stems, and candy. Having received and opened our presents, we would return home and eat a full breakfast, which included bacon, sausage, eggs, fried potatoes, and homemade biscuits. Later, we would go to church for our annual Christmas program, where we would receive "goody bags" (brown paper bags) with special Christmas candies and fruits. After church, we would travel to our maternal grandparents to deliver their gifts and of course, receive ours. They lived in Milford, Virginia, which was about 18 miles from our home. Although my maternal grandparents lived a distance from us, we always visited them on a regular basis and they also visited us.

After Grandma's death, Grandpa Sizer still carried on the tradition of hanging stockings for his grandchildren and providing Christmas treats. All of his children were married and had their own homes. But a close-knit family, a close community, and the proximity of some of his children's homes, allowed him to remain in his home. Within less than a quarter of a mile were three of his sons, their wives, and his grandchildren. Since everyone was within walking distance, different family members would check on him on a regular basis. He was a deacon at the church and also had held the position of superintendent of the Sunday school, so members of the church also visited him on occasion. However, I am sure that during the evenings, while alone at home, he missed Grandma most.

Ancestry

Very little has been disclosed concerning my maternal ancestry. However, throughout the years I heard stories about my paternal great-grandfather and my paternal great-grandmother. I was told that during the Civil War, my paternal great-grandfather, John Karr Sizer, was a sergeant in the Confederate Army, assigned to the 30th Virginia Infantry. His ancestors also fought in the American Revolution and the War of 1812. Reuben Sizer was his father and Catherine Newton Sizer was his mother. His family owned hundreds of acres of land. As a result, John Karr Sizer inherited land. After his death, my paternal great-grandmother, Hawzie Coleman, who had 10 children with him, owned the land. She willed her land to my grandfather, Arthur J. Sizer, and some of his siblings. My grandfather was not only a landowner, he also owned and operated sawmills, sometimes employing as many as 20 men.

I don't remember much about my paternal grandmother, Ina Taylor Sizer, because I was only four or five years old when she died. She appeared to have been about five feet, five inches tall, with an olive complexion and thick hair. She had a large goiter that extended under her chin, from ear to ear, and down her entire neck. When I was young,

I was exposed mostly to my paternal grandfather's family and only knew a few of my paternal grandmother's relatives. However, in the last two years I have met more members of her family (my family) and have acquired a little more information. Her father was Robert Spencer Taylor and her mother, Alberta Carter Taylor. Grandma Sizer had one sister (Virginia) and five brothers (Adolphus, Burton, Ernest, William, and Ephrium who was sometimes called Ethan and was her half brother).

In a letter sent to me in 1992 from Norman Peters, a genealogist and former colleague of mine, the following information based on his research was conveyed: In the 1880 census for the Madison District of Caroline County, residing in the household was John Karr Sizer (48 years old), Hawzie Coleman (30 years old), and six children (Edward J., William H. (Henry), Arthur J., Ann E., Robert W., and Mary J.) with the last name Coleman. I don't know when the Sizer name was assumed by Hawzie's children. My grandfather, Arthur J., was eight years old at the time of the census. Four of his younger siblings (Emily, Ida B., Bertie, and George T.) had not yet been born when this census was taken. Based on the census information, I estimate that Hawzie was born in 1850, 13 years before the Emancipation Proclamation was signed on January 1, 1863. Therefore, I assume she was born a slave. Nevertheless, years later I discovered that Hawzie and her children were identified as servants in the 1880 census. She probably would have been around 18 years old when she conceived her first child.

Hawzie Coleman

John Karr Sizer

John Karr Sizer's Mustache Cup
(in my possession)

John Karr Sizer's 1863 Furlough and Pay Document

Even though the Emancipation Proclamation was supposed to have freed the slaves, they were not allowed many privileges of citizenship. In 1865 the 13th Amendment abolished slavery, but it was not until July 28, 1868, when the 14th Amendment was ratified, that slaves were granted full citizenship and equal protection of the laws.[1] Nevertheless, at that time, it was still illegal for Whites to marry Blacks. It was not until 1967 that this was legal in Virginia.[2] However, each time Hawzie Coleman had a child, John Karr Sizer went to the courthouse and recorded their births, acknowledging that he was the father.

It has been conveyed through oral history that John Karr Sizer would not give up his Colored/Negro family, so he was expelled from his church and not allowed to be buried in the church's cemetery. I was told that he and Hawzie were buried in the forest in the back of the old homeplace. At the time they were buried, it probably wasn't a forest, but the overgrowth in later years made it challenging to locate the graves. However, two family members found the graves in the 1980s, but today none of my relatives who are still alive know their exact location. I have been tempted to contact the White side of our family to see if they know where the graves are, but have not done so as yet.

In 1963, a couple who lived in the same county as I (Caroline County, VA) began to challenge the law in Virginia banning interracial marriage. This involved a White man, Richard Loving, and a Negro woman, Mildred Jeter. In 1958, the couple moved to Washington, DC, in order to get married. When they returned to Virginia, they were arrested, tried, and found guilty of breaking the law that banned cohabitation or marriage of different races and were sentenced to one year in jail. The judge suspended their sentence under the conditions that they would leave the state and not return for 25 years.[3] However, the couple appealed this decision. In 1967 the United States Supreme Court heard the *Loving v. Virginia* case and ruled unanimously in favor of the Lovings. This decision ended the ban on interracial marriage nationwide.

On the grounds of the courthouse in the town of Bowling Green (Caroline County, VA), a monument has been erected recognizing the many historical contributions of African Americans from the county, including the Lovings. My father's name, Frank Chester Sizer, is also engraved on this memorial as the first African American member of the county school board. There is also a plaque on the wall in the courthouse citing the *Loving v. Virginia* case, and in 2018 a marker was placed alongside U.S. Route 301, near the road leading to Central Point, Virginia, where they both grew up.

Central Point, Virginia was the location of my mother's church, St. Stephens Baptist. She was a member of this church until she married my dad, and shortly thereafter she joined Ebenezer Baptist in Chilesburg. St. Stephens Church was the same church that Mildred Loving attended; she was buried in that cemetery. When I was young, I didn't like visiting that church because most of the people there were light-skinned; many looked White. I felt uncomfortable and out of place even though I looked like them. I was more comfortable with my church in Chilesburg, where many members of the congregation were related to me and represented all the different shades of my race. The complexion of St. Stephens today is very different, more diverse.

Throughout my childhood, until I graduated from high school, we would make that long trip to St. Stephens a few times each year. It seemed to have been about 35 miles away from our home in Chilesburg. I think it was my mom's way of keeping in touch with her family and friends. As an adult, I have had occasion to return to St. Stephens. The last time was just a few years ago for my first cousin's funeral. Many of my relatives on my mom's side of the family are buried in the cemetery at St. Stephens Church.

Unlike my father's family, my mother's family never had family reunions. But I spent a lot of time with my maternal grandfather (John W. Richardson) and my maternal grandmother (Clara Beasley Richardson). In the Bowling Green, VA census of 1900, my grandfather's race was recorded as "M" (mulatto). I was told that if the census takers couldn't identify the race of an individual, they just used this as a blanket reference to indicate that they were not White. My grandfather always said he was Irish-Indian. To me, he looked more Irish than Indian (Native American). However, in later years, when I had my DNA tested, it did not reveal any Native American ancestry.

Grandpa Richardson's father was George T. Richardson and his mother was Amanda Pitts Richardson. He had six brothers (Hammie, Grover Cleveland, George, Robert, Bernard, and Dan) and two sisters (Mary and Florence). I only knew his brother, Dan. I remember seeing my great-aunt Florence from a distance when I was young, but I was never physically close enough to her to have a conversation or to recognize her if I ever saw her again. In the 1910 and 1920 censuses of Bowling Green, my grandmother's race was recorded as "M" (mulatto). Grandma Richardson's father was William L. Beasley and her mother was Fannie Clarke Beasley. She had two sisters (Laura and Lillian). I knew her sister, Lillian. I called her Aunt Lil. She was married to my grandfather's brother, Dan. Also, I was fortunate to have spent a little time with my great-grandmother, Fannie.

Grandpa Sizer

When I was about five years old, after my paternal grandmother's death, I would walk to my paternal grandfather's house by myself. Since I lived just two houses away and across the road from him, my parents allowed me to do this. The country roads were not heavily traveled back then and everybody knew everybody, so I wasn't afraid to go at any time. I felt it was my duty and responsibility to keep Grandpa Sizer company after my grandmother's death, so I began a routine. Every morning after my brother and sister left for school, I would leave for Grandpa's house.

Grandpa's house was a large, white, wood-frame house with a front porch that extended over the entire front of the house. It was about 50 yards from the road. Many acres of land with all types of trees surrounded his house. He had peach, plum, apple, and walnut trees. As a matter of fact, the best golden delicious apple tree was right behind the outhouse! There was a smokehouse, a chicken house, and a corn shed. Some days I would sit in the corn shed with a needle and thread, punching a hole through dried corn kernels to make corn necklaces.

Indoor plumbing was not one of the luxuries Grandpa enjoyed. In the kitchen was a refreshing, very cold pail of water for drinking, drawn from the well in the backyard. Believe it or not, everyone in the family drank out of the same dipper. I also remember standing beside the well and drinking water from the bucket with a dipper. There is a sad story connected to one of the wells in the backyard of Grandpa's home. One of my grandmother's brothers was 24 years old when he was suffering from severe delirium caused by typhoid fever, and he committed suicide by jumping into the well. Of course, they had to dig a new well after this tragic event. This happened before I was born.

Since there was no indoor plumbing, during the day we had to go outside to use the toilet. At night, we used chamber pots/slop jars (small porcelain pails with handles and lids), which were placed in different bedrooms throughout the house. In order to fit into the décor and be more visually appealing, there was a nice wooden encasement in which you could place the slop jar. One could sit there and afterwards the slop jar could be concealed by closing the top. In the morning, we had to carry the slop jars to the outhouse to empty them; not the best chore, but necessary.

There was a long driveway that passed near the side of Grandpa's house that formed a circle to guide the cars back to the main road. Inside the circle was a small flower garden, an area with grass, flowers, and small bushes that my grandparents had planted to add to the aesthetic appeal of the driveway. Large stones were placed around the perimeter of the circle to prevent cars from damaging the garden. We often played in this circle, and it was always a choice location to hide eggs during our family's annual Easter egg hunts. I usually entered the house through the side door into an enclosed porch that had about five cement steps leading up to it. Because there was a couch on this porch, it was used as a sitting room. To the right of this room was a doorway leading to a hallway. In this hallway, to the left, was a doorway leading to the living room, which included a fireplace. Before approaching the front door, a large portrait of John Karr Sizer, my grandfather's father, dressed in his Confederate uniform, could be seen on the left wall. A sharp turn to the right would lead to the staircase with that beautiful, wooden bannister. Upstairs were three large bedrooms, one large enough to accommodate two double beds, a dresser, and a chest of drawers. Next to the couch on the side porch was a door leading to Grandpa's bedroom. To the left of the couch was a doorway that led to the dining room. As I walked through the dining room, I would hear the squeaky floor, where each step made the floor move just enough to cause the crystal glasses in the china closet to rattle—this always happened! After leaving the dining room, there was another doorway leading to a large kitchen with a walk-in pantry. Once in the backyard, to the left of the back porch was a door with five or six steps leading down to a cellar. When there was a heavy rain, sometimes two or three feet of water would accumulate, and we would jump into the water for fun.

My grandfather was about 78 years old when Grandma died. His hair was thin and completely gray; his head was partially bald on top. He wore glasses and smoked a pipe. At over six feet tall, at least it seemed like that to me, I always looked up to him, literally and figuratively. He was a deacon at our church. Folks around our part of Virginia were mostly Baptist, especially Black folks. His mother was born a slave, so formal education was not an option for him. I don't know how or when he learned to read, but he was still able to read the Bible and did so every day. I was told he had read the Bible from the beginning to the end at least two or three times.

Discriminatory practices in public school funding after slavery, especially in the South from the late 1800s and even beyond the 1950s, led to the majority of schools for Colored/ Negro students having inferior buildings and supplies and, in some cases, no schools at all. As I mentioned earlier, the 14th Amendment, ratified in 1868, granted citizenship and equal protection of the laws to everyone born in the United States or naturalized, including freed slaves. But the *Plessy v. Ferguson* case of 1896 challenged the 14th Amendment and as a result, it basically legitimized the racial separation that most of the southern states were already practicing. The Supreme Court ruled that racially separate facilities, if equal, did not violate the Constitution and were not discriminatory, resulting in the "separate but equal" decision that perpetuated and justified the segregation of the races.[4] This was known as the "Jim Crow" law. Therefore, throughout the South, there were separate schools, separate restrooms and water fountains in public places, separate cars on trains, etc.

My father attended a one-room church school built just about 30 yards away from his church, Ebenezer Baptist, which was located about two or three miles from his home. His teacher was his oldest sister, Ruth, who received her

Grandpa Sizer's House

teaching certificate from Virginia State Normal and Industrial Institute, which later became Virginia State University. (I think only two years of college were required for a teaching certificate at that time.) During the 1920s and '30s, when my father was growing up, his family did not own a car. Therefore, there was no transportation to travel to the only high school for Colored children, located in Bowling Green, which was about 20 miles from the family home; consequently, my dad's educational opportunities were just a little better than my grandfather's.

There were 13 children in my father's family, and although less than half of them graduated from high school and only two from college, they were all able to own their own homes and support their families. The girls in the family married men who were capable of supporting them, and they worked along with their husbands in order to acquire the necessities and some luxuries for themselves. Due to the fact that there were more opportunities for employment in the cities, many Negroes, including my family members, migrated there. Six of the girls in my dad's family moved to Washington, DC. The one who previously taught in Caroline County moved to Raleigh, North Carolina, for a while with her husband, who was a graduate of Ohio State University and business manager of Shaw University before permanently settling in Petersburg, Virginia. One sister made a permanent home in Richmond, Virginia. (Prior to moving to Richmond, she lived with her sister in Raleigh, NC, in order to attend high school; she married a man who received degrees from Ohio State University and Yale University. Later she received a degree from Shaw University and became a teacher.)

The sisters who moved to Washington, DC, found employment with the city government, federal government, and private sector. They worked as elevator operators, cafeteria workers, domestic workers, and telephone operators. One of these sisters, after the death of her husband, worked as an office cleaner at the White House during the Kennedy administration. After working for years in the federal government, another sister and her husband were able to purchase and operate a motel in Wildwood, New Jersey. This was quite an accomplishment for one who had only an elementary school education. Only one of the five boys moved to Washington, DC, and the others remained in Chilesburg.

Each day when I visited Grandpa, I would sit at his feet next to an old, wood stove in his bedroom where he sat in his special reclining chair. Also in the room was a bed, a dresser with a picture of President Franklin Delano Roosevelt on it (one of his sons' middle name was Roosevelt), and an armoire. On a shelf to the right side of the stove was a small grandfather clock. To the left of his chair was a bookshelf where he kept his Bible. A floor stand placed near the window held his special tobacco and pipes. In the armoire, he always had a quart-size container full of candy, and each time any of his grandchildren visited, he would set us on his knee and allow us to take only one piece. As I sat on his knee, I watched as he spread his big hand around the top of the jar. His fingers had become crooked and the knuckles swollen (probably from arthritis), but he was still able to manipulate the wide-mouth jar. Nonetheless, there were times when I would try to get a second piece, but it seemed that Grandpa would always remember if I had had my limit for that day. My aunts gave me this container after he died. To my surprise, I discovered that it was just an old Yardley jar that may have contained talcum powder or shaving cream, but it was very special to me. The jar was glass with a plastic, ivory-colored top. The top had a small dome in the center with a bumblebee design in each of the four sections; around the dome were the words "Yardley, 33 Bond Street, London." Over 60 years later, I still have that jar.

As I sat at his feet, he would read the Bible to me. The Bible had a lot of pictures in it, and I believe my fear of snakes developed after seeing the picture of Moses pointing to a staff with a bronze/golden serpent wrapped around it. The biblical story, conveyed by Grandpa, was that if people lacked the faith to look at the serpent, they were bitten by snakes as a punishment by God. Later, I had a few encounters of my own with snakes that I haven't forgotten. For many years thereafter, the remembrance of these images would cause me to have nightmares. I would dream of snakes as big as trains slithering in the back of our house just beyond the forest. In another dream, I was Super Girl with a cape draped around my shoulders standing in the middle of a bed with snakes all around me. However, thanks to my "super powers," I was able to fly over them and escape!

In real life I had the following experiences. One day when I was in elementary school, my mom sent me on an errand to deliver a bowl to my aunt who lived next door to us. Since many family members were often going back and forth between the two houses, a path was created. On the way there, I encountered a moccasin snake. It crossed directly in front of me, so I stood still and just started screaming; fortunately, it continued on its way. Another experience that contributed to this fear occurred when I was in the 10th grade in high school. At the top of the stairs on the second floor of our home, there was a small area that divided my room from my two brothers' room; it was large enough for a crib, with room to spare. There were two windows in each bedroom and one in this small area. After my sister left home to attend college, I had a bedroom all to myself. One morning as I was lying in bed, my niece, Debbie, who was about seven months old, began to cry. To avoid having to go back and forth, I took her out of her crib located in this small area and put her in bed with me. At the foot of my bed was a chimney that started downstairs in my parents' bedroom along the back of their wall and continued up through the middle of my room. The space between the ceiling and chimney in my room had not been sealed, so there was a small opening. Debbie and I fell asleep, but when I woke up, I noticed something white extending between the chimney and ceiling. I thought it was just insulation so I went back to sleep. Later when I awakened, I noticed it had become longer, so I decided to check to see what was really going on. To my surprise, I saw two black eyes and the white underbelly of what turned out to be a black snake! I immediately grabbed Debbie and jumped across the bed to the other side of the room, as close to the wall and as far away as possible from the snake. But just as I ran to the doorway, the snake dropped even farther down the side of the chimney. I continued running down the steps and called my mom at work to tell her what happened.

It was a warm summer day and she came home as soon as possible. When we explored upstairs, we discovered the snake had left my room and somehow traveled to my brothers' room and wrapped itself around the top of the Venetian blind at the front window of their room. There was a pool cue in the corner of the room, so my mom grabbed it and pressed it against the snake and told me to hold it. As I pressed down, the snake seemed to hiss or spray something in my face. I don't know if it was moisture or just air. I pressed really hard and Mom began to cut up the snake with a knife. It was a black snake about six feet long. After she finished, she threw it out of the upstairs window where it landed on the ground. That evening, as Daddy was working in the garden in the back of our home, he saw a snake and because he knew she had killed a snake earlier, he asked Mom why she had thrown it in the garden. But it turned out to be another one; they say snakes travel in pairs. Of course, this did not help my fear of snakes diminish. I don't believe Grandpa ever realized the impact that picture of Moses with all those serpents had on me. I never mentioned it to him.

Before reading the Bible, Grandpa would eat breakfast, which almost always included oatmeal. I would watch him eat. Sometimes the oatmeal would slide down his chin from the corner of his mouth. When he drank water, he would have to hold the side of his mouth so it wouldn't spill out. I was told that, in his youth, he had been attacked by a bull and sustained an injury to his mouth. I also heard that he had been struck by lightning. My sister said that he had had a stroke. Whatever the cause, he had a problem with the muscles around his mouth.

Lunchtime would roll around and it seemed like, every day, Grandpa would have toast with grape jelly along with a block of sharp cheddar cheese and crackers. For dinner, he would walk over to Uncle Eddie's house, which was across the road from his house. Some days, if he ran out of something, I would walk to the general store, which was about a half mile away, to get things for him. He would pay me a quarter for doing this. The general store had everything in it: clothes, feed for the animals, meats, vegetables, dairy products, candy, a post office, and it even had a service station with gas pumps. A White couple, Mr. and Mrs. Humphrey, owned the general store, and they always called my grandfather "Uncle Arthur." I thought it was used as a term of endearment, but later I learned that they were not likely to call him Mr. Sizer because Colored people were not given that type of respect.

At the end of each day, when three o'clock rolled around and it was about time for the school bus to bring my brother and sister home, I would spend the longest time preparing for my exit. As I said good-bye to Grandpa, I would ask over and over again, "Are you sure you won't be lonely?" I wouldn't leave until I was convinced he wouldn't be lonely. Even though we were within yelling distance of each other, I still worried about him. I knew he must have missed Grandma. Living in that big, white house with that beautiful, long bannister all by himself, he must have been very lonely.

Grandpa and I would walk to church on a few Sundays. Ebenezer Baptist Church was quite a way down the road, maybe two or three miles. As a child this seemed awfully far, but I loved doing this with Grandpa. Because he was so tall, he'd take one step and I would take two trying to keep up with him.

One Sunday after church I decided to walk up to Cousin Carrie's house. She lived with her mother, Miss Lucy Baber. The main part of the house was built in the 1800s; other rooms were added over time. When I was in elementary school, I was told that one section of it was about 100 years old. During the 1970s, my sister and her husband purchased this house, along with the surrounding nine acres of land, from Cousin Carrie. The old house was painted white with green shutters framing the windows. On the first and second floors, the porches wrapped around the house in an L-shape. It reminded me of the houses you might see in New Orleans. Entering from the front door, as I walked through the hallway, to the left, I always would see a large painting of Lena Horne that covered the entire wall. Her image appeared to be actually designed on the wallpaper. Lena Horne was a beautiful, African American, singer, dancer, actress, and civil rights activist. She was one of the first to achieve nationwide popularity among Whites, as well as Blacks. However, I only remember seeing her on the television as a singer during that time. Many years later, they sold this property to one of our first cousins. Because no one was living there, around 2011 my cousin tore it down as he built his new home about a half-acre from this old house.

I regret not knowing during my childhood that Cousin Carrie was really my grandfather's child and, therefore, my father's half-sister and my aunt. In spite of this, I had a closer relationship with her than with most of my family-acknowledged aunts. If they had known that she was their half-sister, my aunts had managed to keep it a secret. In fact, they did not interact with her very much at all, even though one of them lived directly across the road from her. We attended the same church, as did many of my relatives, yet no one ever let on or hinted that she was my aunt. One day as we drove past Cousin Carrie's house, Daddy said, "She looks just like Arthur Sizer." He didn't explain to me what he meant by that comment, but I was in college and drew my own conclusion. When I mentioned this to my sister, she told me that she found out about this secret many years earlier, during my grandfather's funeral. She noticed that Cousin Carrie was riding in the family limousine. She asked my mother why, and it was at that time my mother revealed that she was Grandpa's child.

I always liked visiting Cousin Carrie's home. She didn't have indoor plumbing either, but what I found to be different than my grandfather's was that she had a water pump on top of her well. She didn't get her water from a well by using a bucket tied to a rope but rather by repeatedly pumping a metal handle until the water came through a spout. I thought it was unique. During that time no one else in the neighborhood had one. For income, she converted one of the rooms of her home into a beauty salon. Her customers were only Black women, and she used hot straightening irons along with hot curling irons to style their hair. I always wanted her to style my hair. Because my hair was very fine and somewhat straight, she said I did not need the heat on it. But I wanted my hair to be thick and curly, so I could get my hair done just like the other customers. Finally, on one special occasion, with my mom's permission, she did.

Cousin Carrie was able to acquire additional income by being a foster parent. She always had children in her home. I looked forward to visiting her and having children my age as playmates. Sometimes there would be two children and other times there might be three or four from the same family. Most of the foster children were girls, but I do remember one boy among a family of four children. Cousin Carrie was a foster parent for 27 children. This was not just a temporary arrangement for her; she nurtured them as if they were her own. Many remained with her for years; one married the brother of a famous professional football player from a football team then known as the Baltimore Colts. I especially remember two sisters whose last name was Loving. I played with them when I was very young, but they left after a short while. They looked as if they were White, so later in life I began to wonder if they were related to the Loving family in Caroline County.

After Grandpa died, Cousin Carrie allowed Fleming Coleman to park his trailer on her property. Fleming had lived in this trailer on Grandpa's land for years. I have been trying to figure out if he was related to us, because my great-grandmother's last name was Coleman. Why else would Grandpa provide a place for him to live? To this day, I cannot recall anyone in the family ever saying anything that acknowledged him as being a relative. He was very dark-skinned and illiterate. On Sundays, he sang in the choir at our church and would hold the hymnal but was unable to actually read it. He worked odd jobs, among them, cutting grass and digging graves. A kind, well-mannered man, he was just a part of our community and everyone seemed to respect him and look out for him.

Anyway, when I got tired of talking to Cousin Carrie on this particular Sunday, I decided to go into the woods between her house and Uncle Eddie's house, where there was a sawdust pile about two stories high. This was residue from a sawmill that Grandpa used to manage. I had on my Sunday clothes: a beautiful, white-lace dress, black patent leather shoes, and white socks with lace around the top. It was summertime, but the sawdust was cool since it was hidden among the trees, so I would go all the way to the top, and lie down on my back and roll all the way to the bottom. I did this until I got tired.

But before I could get home, Cousin Carrie had called my parents and told them that I had gone into the woods; she knew I would be tempted by the cool sawdust pile. Our telephones were connected to party lines and it was my bad luck that no one was using the phone at that moment, so she reached my parents sooner than I expected. (On party lines, several households were connected to the same telephone line and could pick up the phone and hear the conversations of others. If you needed to make a phone call and someone else was using the phone in the neighborhood, you just had to wait until the line was free.) I got one of the few whippings that I can remember on that day. Back then, parents told you not to do certain things, but they seldom told you why you shouldn't do them. I guess if I had been swallowed up by a sinkhole in the sawdust pile, they might have never found me and I would have suffocated. Furthermore, no one knew where I was except Cousin Carrie, and even she wouldn't have known, if it had been up to me.

I got the nickname "Tramp" from my Uncle Arthur because I was never home and was always on the road to Grandpa's, Cousin Carrie's, etc. When he called me "Tramp," I was so embarrassed because of the other connotation of the word. He continued to call me this throughout college and most of my adult life. He also called me "Blinky" because I blinked more than the average person. When I complained to my mother about this condition, she told me that she used to blink when she was a little girl and when her father threatened to spank her if she didn't stop, she stopped. This was not the case for me; nothing made me stop, and nothing was ever done to identify the cause of my blinking. As an adult, I have asked doctors about it but none have provided an adequate explanation, much less a solution.

Uncle Arthur's home was to the right of ours. He had a funny, sometimes obscene name for everyone. He was my dad's brother and his wife, Aunt Lillian, was my mom's sister. We call their children our double first cousins. This marriage combination occurred on both sides of the family. My maternal grandfather and his brother married two sisters, and my paternal grandfather and his brother married two sisters. Simply put, two siblings from one family married two siblings from another family. I guess when they were courting, one brother may have taken his brother along with him for company while traveling, maybe by horse and buggy. Uncle Arthur, like Mom's brothers, had served in the military during World War II and was also scarred by it. When I was young, he drank a lot and cursed like a sailor, even though he served in the army. His son, at a young age, heard him frequently cursing, so I suppose he thought it was a good thing. As a result, there were times that Uncle Arthur, or even some other relatives, would sneak up on his son while he was in the woodshed behind their house and hear him practicing cursing—just like Uncle Arthur! The apple didn't fall far from the tree.

Surviving

My parents were married at a young age; both were 18 years old, but my dad was a few months older than my mom. Within six years, they had three children. I was the third child. They worked very hard to provide for their family, but the time came when there were not sufficient jobs near our home to support our family. As a last resort, during the 1940s and 1950s, my parents worked in Washington, DC. Since my father had sisters who were married and had homes there, I suppose they lived with one of them during the week and would return home on the weekends. They also lived with my mother's cousin in DC for a brief period. My father was a security guard at the Pentagon, and my mother was a waitress at a very popular, well-known restaurant. I don't know what the requirements were for my father's job, but during that time I know that Black women did not hold the position of waitress at that restaurant. My mother would tell us about the comments and jokes the White workers in the restaurant would make while she was working concerning Black people; she had to hold her tongue for fear of them finding out that she was Black since she might lose her job. My mom had straight, fine, brown hair. Her complexion was very fair. She had hazel eyes and a very keen nose. Dad used to tease her about her nose—I thought it looked like Bob Hope's or Richard Nixon's. I was thankful that this was one of her traits I didn't inherit, but I am grateful for the many others that I did.

Because segregation and discrimination still existed in the late fifties and sixties, some girls in my high school had to leave Virginia after graduation in order to pursue their ambitions to become models. I was told that before attending our high school, one of these girls had been expelled from a White school when the principal discovered she was not White, as defined by Virginia law. At one time, Virginia law stated that if you had one-sixteenth of Black blood in you, you were Black. But later they took it to the extreme, declaring that if you had one drop of Black blood in you, you were Black. Of course, this was not based on DNA tests, more on physical attributes. But because she was very fair-skinned, had blonde hair and blue eyes, this girl could pass for White in a city where no one knew her. She became a model in New York City.

While my parents worked in DC, we initially stayed with my maternal grandparents in Milford, Virginia. I always enjoyed staying at Grandpa and Grandma Richardson's home. I remember being allowed to have coffee with breakfast at four or five years old. Of course, my mother would not allow this when we were at home in Chilesburg, but Grandma would put a little bit of coffee in the cup with a whole lot of milk. Grandma usually had coffee with sugar and cream that was taken from the top of the bottled milk that was delivered to their house. They also had a cow, so cream from that milk was also used.

Lucille, Mama, Bootsie, and me (I am on Mama's lap.)

As I entered my grandparents' home through the back door, immediately to the right were a few steps leading to a door that once opened, led to additional steps leading up into the attic. This area provided enough space for two bedrooms, but it also had an old gramophone and other interesting items for me to explore. I slept downstairs in the dining room on the sofa bed. A wood stove was located in this room. Since there was no central heat in their home, wood stoves provided warmth. In the winter, at night after the fire had burned out, it would become very cold. But I could stay in bed in the morning until Grandpa made the fire and Grandma cooked breakfast. The heat of a wood stove is the best feeling when you wake up on a cold morning. In the kitchen there was also a wood stove designed for cooking; it had one side where you could put in the wood, and on the other side was a reservoir for heating water. Grandma could make the best bread using her cast-iron frying pan on top of the stove. We would add molasses and butter on the bread and it was the best thing ever!

Usually after making the fire, Grandpa would drive down to the local store and about the time we were sitting down at the table for breakfast, we would hear his truck as it passed right outside of the kitchen window. He would bring eggs and anything else Grandma needed. I suspect he not only visited with his friends when he went there, but also would have a few drinks. They used to joke about him leaving home white and coming back home red because his face would be flushed after drinking.

Grandpa was a mail carrier during the 1940s and '50s.

I used to watch him hang the mail bag on the hook which was attached to a pole beside the track so the train passing through could pick it up. The train never stopped, but the mail was picked up! During this time, it was rare and very difficult for Colored men to get jobs as mail carriers, but he and his brother had these jobs. I found a picture of him standing beside his truck at a Newtown, Virginia, post office which is located in King and Queen County, Virginia. This may have been just one of his stops along his mail route, but I am sure he also delivered mail in Caroline County where he lived.

In the 1950s, Grandpa used to take us to the beach during the summer months when we were out of school. Sometimes after church on Sundays, he would take us to Mark Haven Beach in Tappahannock, Virginia, along the Rappahannock River, or on a rare occasion to Buckroe Beach, on the eastern shore of Hampton, Virginia, along the Chesapeake Bay. I remember Buckroe being segregated, one side for Blacks and one for Whites. A fence divided the two sections. I don't remember on which side we swam, but there were always several of us grandkids with him. After the 1964 Civil Rights Act was signed by President Lyndon B. Johnson, Buckroe Beach was integrated. The Civil Rights Act of 1964 outlawed discrimination in public accommodations engaged in interstate commerce, including hotels, restaurants, and theaters. It forbade state and local governments from restricting access to public facilities on the grounds of "race, color, religion, or national origin." It also empowered the Justice Department to initiate lawsuits to desegregate schools.[5]

Grandpa Richardson at a young age

Grandpa Richardson on his mail route

Mark Haven Beach, on the other hand, was for Colored folks. My grandfather knew the owner, Reginald Markham. Because my grandfather always had a pickup truck with the bed covered, he had seats in the back that could accommodate several of his grandchildren. On one particular occasion, my cousin Skeeter was with us. I didn't know how to swim but as I stood on the platform or pier, he decided to push me into the water. I landed on my back with water covering my body and face. I panicked because the water was going up my nose and into my mouth. It seemed like forever before I came up out of the water. Ever since then I have had a fear of water, and this has impacted my life in many ways for all these years.

I always took baths; I never took showers at home because I couldn't stand the feeling of water hitting me in my face. It wasn't until college when my only option was to take a shower that I forced myself to do so. In trying to overcome my fear, after I left college, I took three different sets of swimming lessons. Each time there was some progress. I managed to put my head under water during the first few lessons, and I swam across the Olympic-size swimming pool. Because I continued to play the clarinet beyond college, my lungs had developed to the extent that I could hold my breath all the way across the pool, since I also hated the feeling of water splashing in my face when I tried to breathe. During the second lesson, I learned to tread water and I ventured into the deep end of the pool. But one day as I was swimming near the edge of the pool in the deep end, I turned my head sideways attempting to breathe, water hit my face, and I panicked. I threw one hand up and the instructor managed to grab my arm and pulled me straight up out of the water. I landed on my feet on the side of the pool! I guess the last lesson was more of the basics, along with floating on my back. I never really felt comfortable breathing and swimming; therefore, I never became a swimmer.

This swimming-related experience is not so much about me, as about my brother. I was with him one day when we were visiting our cousin who had a pond on his property. My older brother, Bootsie, who was about two years older than I, decided he was going to jump into the pond. My dad yelled at him saying, "Don't go in that water until you learn how to swim!" At the time, the thought occurred to me, "How will you ever learn to swim if you don't go in the water?" Living in the country, there were no swimming pools for us in our neighborhood, or at school, or anywhere nearby. Although the North Anna River was a few miles down the road from our home, no one knew how to swim, so no one could teach anyone how to swim.

Another incident occurred when I was baptized; I was 12 years old. In the Baptist church to which I belonged, when you joined the church, you were baptized in a pond or river, not in a pool inside the church like many are today. This happened only once a year after the church's Revival Week during August. On this particular day, the deacons, deaconesses, and members of the congregation were standing on the banks of the river singing hymns as the ministers walked me down into the water. The minister of my church held one arm and the visiting minister who preached during Revival Week held the other. I, like all the other girls, was wearing a white dress, and as the ministers submerged me backwards into the water, the skirt of my dress ballooned up. Not only did I panic when my face went under, but I also reached to pull my dress down, then I wiped my face. Mistake. The ministers immediately dumped me back into the water because during this ritual, my minister was supposed to wipe my face, not me. Since I wasn't crazy about being put under water in the first place, this was not a pleasant experience for me. Nevertheless, I did want to get baptized, so I knew that I had to do this.

Living with my grandparents while my parents worked in Washington was one means of providing a stable environment for us. But my brother, sister, and I needed to be in a place where we could permanently attend the school assigned to us based on where we actually lived. So my parents were able to find a nice lady named Miss Bessie Clarke (possibly a maternal cousin) who lived near my mother's church, in Central Point or Sparta, Virginia, to stay with us at home in Chilesburg during the weekdays. She had gray hair, wore glasses, and appeared to be in her seventies. She may have been younger, but during that time, anyone over 40 seemed old to me. Sometimes, we gave her a hard time. Once my older brother, who at times had an uncontrollable temper like my father, became angry at me and threw a book. I ducked and just as he threw it, Miss Bessie opened the door behind me, and the book barely missed her. All in all, however, we loved Miss Bessie and she took very good care of us. We missed her when she left.

After the jobs in Washington ended, my mom became a

housewife again and my dad began working at the Sylvania Plant (FMC Corporation) in Fredericksburg, Virginia. At that time, we had an old, used 1939 Chevrolet. My sister told me that at night, Dad would put an old army blanket over the hood of the car, and drive it up close to the house so that the water in the radiator wouldn't freeze. Doing this meant that he would spend less money on anti-freeze. Daddy's job was about 30 miles away. Fortunately, the men in our neighborhood were transported to work and back by a bus the company provided.

St. John
Elementary School

In February 1952 I turned six years old and could finally go to school the next September just like my sister and brother. State law required us to be six years old by a certain date before we could begin first grade. Since I did not qualify by this particular date, I was always older than most of the students in my class. Many of them would still be six when I would turn seven during that first year of school.

Early in the morning, before the sun came up, we would wake up, get dressed, eat breakfast, and walk over a half mile to catch the bus to school. At six years old, this seemed like a long walk. The bus picked us up at the Humphreys' General Store. The store was located on an incline at a fork in the road, one road leading to Spotsylvania County and the other to Hanover County. Anyone in our county who lived in either direction beyond this point had to walk to this location. Of course, during that time it was just my family that lived in the direction of Hanover County and the Brown family that lived in the other direction toward Spotsylvania County. A few years later, after my father complained and threatened to enroll us in the White school, C. T. Smith Elementary, which was closer to our home, the route was changed so that the bus actually turned around in our driveway. As more of my cousins who lived farther away from the General Store in the direction of Hanover County reached school age, the bus route was changed again to accommodate the new students. Of course, the bus stopped in front of our home.

Our bus had to travel a specific route, which was not very direct, in order to pick up all of the Colored students in the different neighborhoods. Most of the roads were crooked and a few were unpaved dirt roads. We rode about 12 miles one way to our elementary school even though the White school was only five miles from our home. Located in Ladysmith, C. T. Smith Elementary was a large brick building with several classrooms, and it probably had central heating and indoor plumbing.

In 1952, the schools in Virginia were still segregated. My first school was St. John Elementary, a two-room schoolhouse with wood stoves. There were outdoor toilets/outhouses about 30 yards behind the school, a set of swings and a merry-go-round to the right. St. John Elementary, now a residence, was a wood-frame structure with two steps leading up to the porch. Each classroom had its own entrance from the porch. The door to the left was for the primary classroom (grades 1–3) the door directly in front of the steps was for the intermediate classroom (grades 4–7). The front yard where we played games such as hopscotch, dodgeball, and jump rope was mostly dirt. There were three tables in the primary room—one for first grade, one for second grade, and one for third grade. My brother and sister also attended this school. The intermediate classroom had rows of armchairs, one row for each grade level. We had to bring our lunches

St. John Elementary was a two-room school with
grades 1–7. Now it is a residence.
(Picture taken in 2010)

to school. I cannot recall if we got our water for drinking from a well or not. But I do recall bobbing for apples during Halloween, so there must have been some source of water. There were no kindergarten, middle, or junior high schools in our county at the time. Elementary school included first through seventh grade and high school was eighth through twelfth. When I entered first grade, the required vaccinations were administered at the school by a visiting nurse. These were the only ones I received, with the exception of the polio vaccine, once it became available. I may have been in the fourth grade. But in order to receive that, we had to stand in a long line on a very hot day, at a special location in Bowling Green, the county seat. I spent three years at St. John.

One incident that occurred when I was in the first grade at St. John involved a girl who asked to comb my hair because she saw my cousin combing it. School had been dismissed for the day and we were waiting for the bus. She was also in the first grade; she was dark-skinned and had very curly hair. Because I wouldn't let her comb my hair, the next day she made up a story and told it to the principal, Mr. Roots. She told him that she was walking to the toilet and I was standing by a tree and I called her a "son of a bitch." I didn't even know the phrase, much less what it meant. Mr. Roots called us into his classroom on the intermediate side. My sister, Lucille, was probably in the fourth grade and was also one of his students. I remember her crying and begging Mr. Roots not to beat me. I was just standing there looking at him and he kept saying, "Go get a switch, go get a switch." I never moved, I just stood there looking at him because I really didn't understand what was going on. As Lucille continued crying and pleading, Mr. Roots finally gave up and instructed us not to play together anymore. Of course, the next morning we were jumping rope together and having fun again.

Before I had a chance to be promoted to the intermediate classroom at St. John, we were transferred to Balty Elementary School. I don't know why we were transferred; it could have been because of over-enrollment at St. John or because the boundaries for our schools had changed. Since I had heard such bad stories about the new school, I didn't want to go there. The same bus that we rode to St. John also transported us to Balty, but it was just a little farther away from home. I remember crying when my teacher, Miss Crutcher, told me that I was being transferred. I really liked her in spite of the fact that when I was in third grade, she gave me my first whipping, and the last whipping I would ever receive by a teacher. I only got three lashes. I had already begun crying by the time she got to me because we were warned by our parents that if we ever got a whipping at school, we would get a worse one at home. We were passing notes in class and one girl wrote something profane in hers; Miss Crutcher had found it in the ash pan underneath the wood stove. The girl really got a whipping because Miss Crutcher said she was the ringleader. I was terrified because Daddy could really give you a whipping, so much so that Mama would stand by and tell him, "Chester, that's enough." I don't remember, however, if I received another whipping from Daddy for that incident at school. Maybe no one told him. Sometimes, it seemed as though once Daddy started whipping us, he would just get angrier and angrier, until he would lose control. I must say, however, that I can count the number of my whippings on one hand, and I can also recall exactly what I had done to deserve them.

On two other occasions we received whippings, and I do mean WE. Dad would whip all three of us—me, my sister, and my older brother, one after the other because usually all three of us had done the same wrong thing. Our parents would tell us not to leave the house when they left to go grocery shopping, but of course, we did on at least two occasions that I remember. We went up the road to Aunt Ruth's home—we figured that since she was his sister, it wouldn't count. Boy, were we wrong! Dad came up there and got us. With his belt, he helped us find our way back home. After our whipping, we tried to be smart by applying bandages to our welts; because we were fair-skinned, they were pretty obvious. When he saw this, he whipped us until we took them all off! On another occasion, we were visiting our maternal grandparents and were told not to leave the house. This time, we walked up the road to the barber's house and again Dad found us. I remember running down the road trying to stay in front of Dad, but by the time we got to Grandma's house, he had caught up with us. Crawling under the kitchen table still didn't keep me from getting my share of the whipping.

Another funny, yet dangerous time was when Dad told us to turn out the lights upstairs in our bedroom and go to sleep. This was at our home in Chilesburg. He and Mom had a bedroom downstairs. So in order to conceal the light from the lamp, we put one of my brother's undershirts on the shade. Eventually the shirt caught fire; we called Dad. He came upstairs barefoot, not knowing what was happening, and ended up stomping out the flames. After putting out that fire, he started another fire on our behinds! According to today's standards, his corporal punishment might be considered child abuse. But I didn't and still don't see it that way because I think that was the way he had been disciplined; therefore, it was the only way he knew how to discipline. I will admit now, however, I wish he had known another way.

Balty
Elementary School

B alty School was a white, wood-frame building resting on an incline in the yard with a little bit of grass sprinkled around an otherwise dirt yard. The front of the school rested on stilts. The front porch was about six feet off the ground, but the rear of the building was level with the ground. Planks of wood supported the railing, which extended three-quarters across the front of the building; the planks on the floor of the porch were spaced so you could see right through each of them. Sometimes boys would run under the porch and look up girls' dresses. To the left, where the railing ended, was the door to the intermediate classroom, grades 4–7. To the right of that door was the primary classroom door, grades 1–3. Kindergarten was still not offered to us during these years. Only trees and the road were visible from all around the school. Within maybe less than a quarter of a mile in each direction were houses and the local post office. Most of us, however, rode the bus to school as far as 15 miles.

Positioned in the far corners of both rooms were large wood stoves. Both stoves were connected to the same chimney, providing warmth during the cold days. Air conditioning was not an option during the hot days. I don't believe any of us had it in our homes; fans were used. There was also a partition between the two rooms that could be opened to connect or combine the two classrooms. The outdoor toilets (outhouses) were about 40 yards away from the building, set back in the woods with paths leading to them; one for the girls and one for the boys. To the right of the building were swings, a sliding board, and a see-saw. A set of monkey bars was located farther down on the side of the yard between the road and the school.

My fourth-grade year at Balty School, which was my first year there, was one of the most unpleasant of my life! Students of my complexion were in the minority at this school and I don't think many of the other students, nor their parents, had been exposed on a regular basis to a lot of people who looked like me. Therefore, I was subjected to name-calling, bullying, and physical abuse. Some of the children were very poor and some behaved in obscene ways. The first time I ever heard the word "incest" or realized what it meant was at Balty; I had been told about a girl who lived in that neighborhood who had been subjected to this.

Sometimes, during recess, boys would sneak behind the school and smoke. One day I saw my older brother, who was in the sixth grade at the time, smoking a cigarette with some of his friends. That evening as we sat at the dinner table, I had no intention of telling on him, but being young and naïve, I looked at my brother, Bootsie, and said, "Should I tell him?" And of course, my dad immediately said, "Tell me what?" Need I say anything further? Bootsie got a good whipping, so I guess the boys at Balty weren't the only ones with bad habits.

It was often the case that girls could not go to the outhouses without some boy chasing or touching them inappropriately. Many times I would canvass or scope out the area or get a running start when I went to the outhouse/toilet. Inside, there would be a seat with two round holes carved out where you could sit. There was no privacy. Often there would be another girl sitting right beside you with no partition at any level.

During those days, teachers did not supervise students at recess like they are required to do today. On one particular day during lunchtime, a group of girls and I decided to go into the forest to a field that was a distance from the school to pick some apples from a tree. Not far from the girls' outhouse was an old path that seemed to have initially been made by a car or tractor. We went down that path, back into the woods to a clearing where there was a cornfield, an apple tree, and an old, dilapidated house. Before we could get to the apple tree, all of a sudden, a group of boys appeared behind us. We scattered. Some girls ran toward the dilapidated house, others back toward the school, and still others into the cornfield. I was close to the cornfield and thought that since the stalks were high, they would hide me. But one of the boys was able to set his eyes on me and began to chase after me through the cornfield. For a while I was able to evade him, but then I tripped and fell face-down. He immediately jumped on top of me. As scared as I was, I still managed to turn sideways and with the force of my body and elbow, I pushed him off me and proceeded to run back to school. He chased me all the way, and when I reached the playground, I was crying and hyperventilating. I don't remember if I told my teacher or if she found out from someone else, but as a result, he was suspended from school and sent to a reformatory. I really felt bad, thinking this incident was the reason for such drastic punishment, but later I found out that he had been involved in other incidents similar to this. I guess this had been the last straw.

Another incident involved a boy who was old for his grade, very dark-skinned, and rode my school bus. He also lived a long distance from school. One day my teacher, who was also the principal, called a parents' meeting during the school day at lunchtime, and after the meeting my mother must have offered to drive this boy's mother home. She was also very dark-skinned with very short, curly hair. As we were standing on the porch, his mom got in the car with my mom. When he saw this, he became enraged, so he grabbed me, held me backwards over the edge of the porch railing, and threatened to drop me. The porch was about six feet off the ground and the railing added maybe four more feet. I was crying and pleading; he eventually let me go after another boy intervened. I didn't understand why he did this to me; he had never been mean to me before. Years later I figured it out. I finally decided that he may have been embarrassed and that he needed to show the other children that he was not friends with someone who looked like me. I believe this was another situation that occurred as a result of my complexion.

In the wintertime we would have to go into the forest and gather wood for the stoves and pile it up under the porch. We usually did this after school was dismissed and before the bus would come from the high school in the afternoon. The same bus picked up all the Colored kids on our side of the county and delivered us to three elementary schools and one high school, passing by an elementary school for White students. This elementary school was less than five miles away from many of our homes.

We seldom missed days from school because of bad weather. Even when roads were flooded because of hurricanes or bad thunderstorms, we still rode the bus to school. The bus driver, when approaching or driving through water, would determine if it was too risky to continue based on the depth of the water. I have seen the water come up to the first step of the school bus before the driver decided to stop. He/ she would just back up, turn around, and find another route to school. This was especially true of the river that flowed under the bridge near Milford. The river would rise and flood about a quarter or half mile up the road. One day in 1954, Hurricane Hazel hit our neighborhood after we had arrived home from school. I remember hanging on to the back-porch screen door while standing at the top of the porch steps, trying to keep from being blown away by the wind. We were out of school for a few days because of the loss of electricity/ power. When there was no electricity, we would sometimes sit in the dark for hours; at that time, we had oil lamps or candles to use during an emergency. Sparks would fly from the fuse box in the kitchen when lightning struck nearby. We used to unplug all of the electrical appliances, such as the refrigerator, stove, etc. We did not watch TV or operate any other electrical objects during the thunderstorms for fear of them being damaged or even worse, one of us being struck by lightning. Old folks used to say, or it was an old wives' tale, that milk would sour/spoil during a thunderstorm. Did they forget about the fact that people unplugged the refrigerators?

There were times during the winter months when it snowed that our school bus would slide off the road and get stuck in a ditch. I remember staring out of the foggy windows with the bus tilting sideways wondering when or if anyone would come to help. The bus would usually get stuck on one of the backroads where there was little or no traffic. Sometimes it was hours before anyone would pass through or come to our rescue. There were no phones or shortwave radios on the bus or at the elementary schools, so until someone realized that our bus had not arrived at the high school, we were just stuck out there in the cold.

One winter when I was in high school, there was a blizzard and we were out of school for over a week. Since there was no electricity, not only were we unable to have lights or watch TV, but also because we had an electric stove, we couldn't cook our meals. Fortunately, Dad had built a room connected to our garage that was about 12 yards away from our house. The room was furnished with a table, chairs, a sofa, and a bed, but most importantly of all, there was a wood stove that kept us warm. Dad and Mom prepared our meals; they cooked most of the food on this wood stove in a large, cast-iron frying pan, which enhanced the flavor of the food. We spent most of our days out in this room, returning to the house occasionally to retrieve some items. By this time there were only four of us living at home: Mom,

Dad, Ronnie (my baby brother), and me. My older brother, Bootsie, after graduating from high school, joined the Air Force and my older sister, Lucille, was living in Washington, DC. Even though initially this was an exciting venture, after a while it got to be old and we were eager to return to our home and school.

One day at Balty, I was sitting in the first chair of the fourth-grade row next to the wood stove trying to get warm after a long, cold bus ride to school. All of a sudden, a boy grabbed my arm, pulled me up out of my seat, and placed the inside of my arm on the pipe of the stove! The fire had just been made and the stove was very hot, so hot that the pipe was red—I was in so much pain. A blister formed immediately. It began at my right wrist and continued up my arm about five or more inches. The scar stayed on my arm for years. To this day, I have not figured out why he did this. We had not had any interaction prior to this during that morning. We were in the same grade; maybe I had ignored him and he wanted my attention. Maybe he liked me, but this was a strange way of showing it. I just couldn't imagine why he would do this to me, was it just out of pure meanness? I hadn't done or said anything to him.

At the time of the incident, our teacher was sitting at her desk, which was a short distance from the stove. I know she must have seen this, and surely she heard me screaming and crying. Since the teacher did not punish him for this, my mother wrote a note requesting her to administer the appropriate punishment. Still, nothing was done. The teacher was a little overweight; she may have been a substitute teacher. To me, she seemed a little lazy because she never moved from her chair; she sat behind her desk during the entire time she was teaching. Later I discovered that she was pregnant, but that shouldn't have been an excuse. I felt she didn't really have her students' best interest at heart, that she was just biding her time. She didn't remain at our school very long after that. As time passed, in her absence, we had another substitute. Then, Miss Upton arrived at Balty School.

Miss Upton

Miss Alma Upton was a tall, dark-skinned, middle-aged lady who was paralyzed on the entire right side of her body. She told us that she had suffered a stroke. A brace was affixed to her right leg; the clatter of the metal could be heard as she walked across the floor at Balty School. At times she would have to use her left arm to raise her right arm. Learning to speak and write again required long periods of therapy and had been quite a challenge for her. In spite of this, her penmanship was beautiful, even with her left hand, and she was determined that we would shape the cursive letters exactly as instructed and demonstrated. I remember becoming tired of practicing cursive writing. This was fourth grade, but I had actually learned to write cursive by copying my mother's grocery lists at home long before that; she also had beautiful handwriting. To me, it seemed that all of the women in my mom's family had nearly the same style of handwriting; maybe when they were in school, they were taught by the same teacher or someone who required that they duplicate their style of writing, too. I doubt if they had a handwriting book; we didn't. Miss Upton would write the letters on the blackboard and we would copy from that. The cursive alphabet was also displayed above the length of the blackboard.

We seldom had new reading books or textbooks for the other subjects. Back then, we had to buy our own books; sometimes they were used and passed down to us from the White school. We also bought books secondhand from students who had completed that particular grade. On occasion, we would see writing in them by previous owners. (The books from the White school would sometimes have the word "nigger" written in them.) Some were torn and some even had pages missing. I especially remember reading a book entitled *Little Black Sambo*. In fourth grade I didn't realize the implications of this book. I understand now that the main character was supposed to have been a boy from India, but the illustrations in the book depicted a black-skinned character with a big mouth, curly hair, white teeth, and big eyes. To me, this illustration was stereotyping the Black character in a disparaging way. In some instances, in real life, Whites would call Coloreds/Negroes "Sambos," and I believe that it was because of how this character had been depicted in that book.

Miss Upton commuted from Norfolk, Virginia, for a while. But eventually she rented a room from a family in the community. Most of the elementary teachers, as I recall, were not from our county. They were from places like Spotsylvania County, VA; Richmond, VA; or Washington, DC. Many of them eventually ended up living in the community during the week and returning home on some weekends. There weren't many other Black folks in our county of my parents' generation who were afforded the opportunity to attend college, or even graduate from high school. My mother was fortunate to have lived near the high school. She and all her siblings (she had two sisters and two brothers) graduated from Union High in Bowling Green, the same high school that every other Black person in the county attended once transportation was provided for students. Unlike my mother, my father lived approximately 20 miles from the high school and probably only completed fifth or sixth grade. A handful of his 12 siblings graduated from high school. Two attended college, only because they were able to live with someone else. Once, my paternal grandmother sent two of my aunts away to live with a lady in Spotsylvania County, Virginia, to attend high school, but they were treated so badly, undernourished and verbally abused, that Grandma demanded they be sent back home.

The "separate but equal law" was still in effect, but many things were far from equal when it came to the education of Negro children. My father attended a one-room church school, built by the church because the state did not provide sufficient funds for schools for Colored children at that time, from what I understand. We used to play on the porch of that school after Sunday School. By then, however, it had been closed; we were never able to go inside.

Anyway, back to Miss Upton. My parents were operating a restaurant and were commuting each day from our home to the restaurant, which was located about 14 miles away. My fourth-grade year was one that no child would want to experience. My teacher actually lived with us! When my parents weren't home, Miss Upton acted in their stead. At home, Miss Upton would try to manage the four of us kids. My older sister really didn't seem to be impacted by this because my parents would place her in a position of authority as well. But my older brother, Bootsie, had quite a temper and would argue with Miss Upton whenever she would tell us to do something that he didn't agree with. He also attended Balty and was in the sixth grade. I guess it was hard for him, too. One argument occurred the evening before we were scheduled to go on a school field trip. My brother was standing in the hallway at the top of the stairs and Miss Upton was in the hallway at the bottom next to the bedroom where she slept, arguing about how much money we could spend on the field trip to Mount Vernon, Virginia, the home of George Washington. My parents had given each of us five dollars, but Miss Upton said we could only spend 50 cents. She and Bootsie argued back and forth for a while. He told her he was going to spend whatever he wanted to spend; I don't remember what really happened.

Another challenge for Miss Upton was my baby brother, Ronnie, who at age four wasn't old enough to attend school. In the mornings we would have to get him dressed and walk him next door to Aunt Lillian's house to stay during the school day. Many mornings he refused to let anyone dress him. But I remember watching Miss Upton, with her one hand and one leg, wedge him between the commode and wall while putting on his clothes. She could do with one side of her body paralyzed what we couldn't do with both sides of ours.

Growing up in the South during segregation, when prayer and corporal punishment were allowed in the public schools, there were many things that happened which would be frowned upon today. For example, Miss Upton would line us up in the mornings, check our teeth to see if they had been brushed, check our fingernails for cleanliness, and check our ears for wax; we had to raise our arms to see if there was an odor, and even had to take off our shoes to see if our socks were clean. I am sure this was very embarrassing for those students who came from very poor homes because sometimes their socks would have holes in them. She would correct the situation or make provisions for students whenever she found things unacceptable. Although she was paralyzed, the 15- and 16-year-old seventh-grade boys did not try to take advantage of that. They respected her because she commanded respect. Before Miss Upton, they got away with a lot of stuff. But when she would punish them (maybe whack their hands with a ruler), they would just stand there and take it. There were no social promotions when I was in school; the older boys usually dropped out after seventh grade. I guess they were ashamed to go to high school because they were so far behind the other students their age. There may have been a few girls that had been retained, but the boys seemed to be more prevalent. There were no school psychologists, remedial reading specialists, or special education classes available at our school during those years.

In the intermediate classroom at Balty, there was one row with six to ten desks for each grade (4–7). One advantage of having this arrangement was that when I finished my fourth-grade assignments, I could listen to the other lessons for the other grades. Another thing that I remember about Miss

Upton is that she taught us a lot of songs. She also used music to get our attention when we were a little unruly. Sometimes when we were too noisy, she would grab her right arm with the left hand, hold it close to her and just start singing! That would really get our attention. At first, we thought she was a little weird, but eventually we got the message and began to respond.

While in the fourth grade we had to learn all three verses of the Negro National Anthem ("Lift Every Voice and Sing") by memory. In high school, when we were practicing for our graduation program, our principal told us we couldn't graduate unless we knew it. Of course, this was just to motivate us. I learned over time that it was originally a poem written in 1900 by James Weldon Johnson to celebrate Abraham Lincoln's birthday at a segregated Black school in Jacksonville, Florida, and was later set to music in 1905 by his brother, John Rosamond Johnson. After realizing its popularity and impact it had on people, it was adopted by the NAACP (National Association for the Advancement of Colored People) as the Negro National Anthem.[6] One weekend upon returning from her home in Norfolk, Virginia, Miss Upton brought back a pre-band instrument called the Tonette (similar to the recorder) as a gift for me. This was my first musical instrument and may have been what motivated me to join the band in high school and later teach instrumental music.

While living with us, Miss Upton would insist on me washing my socks and underwear during the week, but I refused and told her that my mother washed my clothes. I lost my privilege at school of going to the post office about a quarter of a mile up the road from the school and received a low grade in Health because I wouldn't wash my clothes. I remember her checking the place on the report card that said "Does not respect authority." She would punish us at school for what we didn't do at home and vice versa. I will admit, however, that I learned a lot from Miss Upton; I think I may have learned more in fourth grade than any other grade during my elementary years.

Eventually, after a year with Miss Upton, my parents decided to move the family into the living quarters in the back of our family restaurant. My father continued to work his shifts at the Sylvania Plant in Fredericksburg, Virginia, which was approximately 30 miles away from the restaurant.

Sizer's Place

My parents named the restaurant Sizer's Place, after my family's last name. It was previously named Beverly's Grill. They leased it from the Beverlys, another Black family. Mr. Beverly taught math and science at Union High School and his wife taught at Union Elementary School. Over time, our families became very good friends.

While living at the restaurant, sometimes I would visit my friend Nickie who lived in Ruther Glen, Virginia. Her family's home was located a few miles away from our restaurant. It was a large, four-bedroom house surrounded by acres of land. The houses in their neighborhood were scattered and spaced farther apart than ours in Chilesburg. Sometimes I would spend the night. We would lie in bed talking and giggling until the wee hours of the morning. At that age (10 or 11), for some reason, everything was funny. We couldn't stop giggling. When her mom would admonish us to go to sleep, this seemed to make us giggle even more. We would pull the covers over our heads to muffle the sound, but eventually we would get tired and fall asleep.

One morning after spending the night there, Mr. Beverly and his father (we called him Ol' Man Beverly to distinguish him from his son, Mr. Beverly, the teacher) came to take me home, back to the restaurant. After I got in the car, Mr. Beverly told me that Grandpa Sizer had died. I knew he had been very sick, but I wasn't prepared for this. What hurt even more was that Ol' Man Beverly said, "He was old and we all got to go someday." I was too young to understand what he was saying; this made me cry and hurt even more. Now that I am older, I understand this all too well.

The restaurant, or the grill, as we sometimes called it, was located on Route 1, near Carmel Church and about 30 miles north of Richmond, which at the time was the main corridor from Florida to Maine. Interstate 95 had not been constructed yet, so you can imagine that there was a lot of traffic passing by our restaurant. There were sleeping quarters in the back of the restaurant; a bedroom for Mom and Dad, a bedroom with two twin beds for me and my sister, Lucille, and my brothers, Bootsie and Ronnie, slept in a long hallway in two twin beds. We also had a TV in that hallway. The bathroom with indoor plumbing was off this hallway. Our restaurant provided the kitchen and dining room to complete our new home. There was also a nice-sized yard behind the restaurant where we could play. Several yards away from the restaurant was an outhouse for the customers. Monday through Saturday we would reside there, and on Saturday nights we would return to our home in Chilesburg. We would attend Sunday School and church on Sundays. Dad was still working at the plant in Fredericksburg and along with the income from the grill, he was able to buy our first new car. It was a black-and-white 1957 Chevrolet. From that point on, we had new cars every few years. Mom always wanted a Cadillac, but she

Daddy and his brand-new 1957 Chevrolet

died before getting one. Nevertheless, they were able to buy a white 98 Oldsmobile. We were always a one-car family, and fortunate to be that.

A large sign advertising Coca-Cola and our restaurant was placed alongside the highway near our restaurant that read "Sizer's Place, For Colored." At that time, we were referred to as Colored or Negro, not Black or African-American. (Our birth certificates also list us as Colored.) This was necessary because there were few places Colored folks could stop to eat while traveling, especially in the South. At times a bus load of migrant workers would pass through and stop to eat. This was great for business, but we had to really work hard and fast to accommodate them. Also, directly across the highway in front of our restaurant was a truck stop where Black truck drivers were required to go to the back door in order to be served; they could not sit or eat inside. They did not have to be subjected to that when they came to our restaurant, so this was another source of business. All of us except my baby brother, Ronnie, who was only five years old, contributed to the operation of the restaurant. Even though I was just in the fifth grade, I cooked, waited on tables, operated the cash register, helped clean the restaurant, etc. I hate making potato salad to this day because on weekends, I had to make big containers of it to sell to the customers. Daddy was able to get a beer license, so on the weekends especially, this attracted the locals, who would sometimes drink too much and get very rowdy. We had a lot of patrons on weekends; the parking lot would overflow and cars would have to park alongside the highway. Guys would race cars; on a few occasions, fights would break out, sometimes brother against brother. In order to alleviate this, a couple of times we had to call the police. But all in all, things were usually peaceful and most of the time people were treated with respect.

Some funny things also happened there. My dad was afraid of mice. One morning while he was in the restaurant, we heard him yelling, "Fannie! Fannie!" When we got into the front of the restaurant, we saw him standing on the counter asking Mama to kill a mouse. He said that they made his skin crawl. I guess he felt about mice the way I feel about snakes. Mama was good with a rifle too. On one occasion, I watched her shoot a rat off the trash pile that was a distance from the restaurant. Of course, she didn't shoot the mouse that Daddy saw; I have forgotten if she saw it again after Dad called for her.

Another crazy thing happened, although it wasn't very funny then, but it sounds funny now when I tell the story. I had a green-and-yellow parakeet named "Prettyboy." I kept him in our living quarters and would release him from his cage sometimes. Once, he flew outside and it was not until the next day that I found him in a tree. But the craziest thing happened on another morning after I let him out of his cage; he flew into the kitchen of the restaurant. The cooking grill was nice and hot with grease, ready to cook hamburgers or whatever. There was an exhaust fan in the window next to the grill. Prettyboy flew over and landed on the exhaust fan. Since I was afraid he would get sucked into the fan, I knocked him off and as a result, he landed on the hot, greasy grill. I started crying. I turned around and knocked him off

Inside Sizer's Place, 1957: (L-R) Mildred Rock
(a friend of the family who also worked at the restaurant),
Mama, Daddy, me, and my sister, Lucille

Ronnie, the baby of the family, in front of
our restaurant drinking a soda

the grill. His feet had been fried. I put Vaseline on his feet and wrapped them with bandages. As he stood on his perch, he seemed to be lifting his feet up and down trying to ease the pain of resting them on his perch. He survived this incident!

Before the parakeet, cats were my choice of pets. Sometimes I would have a mother cat and four of her kittens. There was a time that my father put some of them in a sack and took them away; I don't really know what he did with them. In the country, pets like cats and dogs stayed outside. We didn't keep animals in the house; they stayed in the garage or in sheds during the cold weather. Once I had a yellow kitten; I guess this kitten was too young to tolerate the cold weather. As a result, when I picked it up one freezing morning, it was as stiff as a board! I am sure that if I had realized this was going to happen, I would have tried to do something differently to prevent this. I loved all my kittens and cats, so this death, in particular, hurt me a lot because of the way it died. A couple of my cats were killed by cars.

It was bad enough that I cried when I would lose my cats, but to make matters worse, my older brother, Bootsie, and older sister, Lucille, would taunt me by staging funerals on the hillside in the back of our house. They would put the cat in a box, dig a grave, preach a long sermon, and bury it. After a while I no longer wanted cats because it hurt so much when they died.

Bootsie and Lucille not only taunted me about the cats, they teased me about other things too; sometimes they would call me vampire because my hair was long, straight, and stringy. They would gang up on me and tease me so much that one morning I decided to run away from home because I felt so bad—this was before I had started elementary school. Everyone was asleep as I tiptoed down the steps past my parents' bedroom and out the back door. I went up the hill behind our house near the edge of the woods where there was an apple tree. I sat there, leaning with my back up against the tree, wondering when or if anyone would realize that I had left home or missed me. Suddenly an apple fell from the tree and hit me right on the top of my head. There were wasps/bees on the apple and they got tangled in my hair. Since my hair had not been combed yet, they stung and stung until they could get free of my hair. I ran back home, crying, and my head, of course, aching. My parents just thought I had gone outside as usual. No one ever knew that I had run away.

When we lived at the grill, we caught the school bus to the assigned school in that boundary. Mr. Beverly was the bus driver. Since he was a mathematician, he would calculate the speed he needed to drive and the time required for students to board the bus at the various stops in order to get to school by nine o'clock. He would drive accordingly. Sometimes the high school boys would wait until the bus began moving and hop on the bus just as it was pulling off. The boys seemed to enjoy this; I guess they saw this as a challenge. We caught the bus in front of the restaurant for about a 14-mile ride. I attended fifth and sixth grades at Union Elementary, which was right across the field from Union High School, where I would later attend, along with all the other Negro children in the county. Believe me, Union Elementary was a big improvement over the two-room Balty School. It was a larger, wood-frame building with two stories and maybe six or eight classrooms. This school was part of a campus that included a high school, an elementary school, a cannery, and even a building in which a few of the faculty members resided. There was a separate classroom for each grade, fourth through seventh, with approximately 25 or more students in each. We changed classes for the different subjects. At Balty, all of the intermediate grades, fourth through seventh, were in one room. We were assigned to a single row based on our grade and sat there the entire day except for recess and lunchtime. At Union Elementary, we didn't have to bring in firewood; however, we still had to use the outhouse because there wasn't indoor plumbing at this school, either.

Since all of the bus routes originated from the high school after dismissal, I could get on one bus to go home and another to go to the restaurant. One evening before we began living at the restaurant, without my mother's knowledge, I decided to catch the bus to the restaurant. Dad was working at the plant that evening; he worked different shifts. There was a truck driver who had become friends with my mother and father, and this night remained in the restaurant after closing. Mom sent me to the car to wait until she locked the doors to the restaurant. I waited a long time for her to come. Because it was dark and cold in the car, after a while I decided to go see what was taking her so long. When I approached the door, the lights were out; only the lights from the cars passing on the highway and the lights outside were shining into the restaurant. I leaned into the glass door and used my hand to block the exterior light from one side of my face so

I could see. The counter was L-shaped with the cash register midway the longest side and bar stools spaced at intervals in front, along the counter. At the far end of the counter, I saw something that made my heart sink.

I became very nervous and afraid. In the shadows I saw my mother in the arms of the truck driver. I never told anyone about this. I kept it a secret for many years. It was not until after my mother's death that I told my sister, and I have never mentioned it again until now, as you are reading this book. I knew my dad had been unfaithful to my mom before and after this incident, but I never witnessed him doing so. My mother and father both had faltered in their marriage, but in spite of this, I believe they loved each other. My mother never knew that I saw her that night.

For seventh grade, I returned to Balty School, where Miss Upton was still teaching but living with another family in our community. This would be my final year of elementary school. Since I was older and most of the bullies had graduated, there was less teasing and name-calling. When I was in fourth grade, the other kids would tell me that I didn't belong at that school and that I should go to C. T. Smith Elementary School, the White school. They also called me White; I was afraid to call them Black. My mother had told us not to call anyone Black. At that time, calling someone Black was an insult, especially if you weren't dark-skinned yourself. At some point during elementary school, I decided that when I got married, I would marry a brown-skinned man so that when I had children, they would be brown, and people would not have to wonder if they were Black or

White. Then, perhaps, they wouldn't have to go through the bullying and harassment that I encountered as a child.

I experienced prejudicial treatment on a daily basis because of society's Jim Crow laws, so I felt I was being discriminated against not only from outside of my race, but also within my race. On a more personal level, an incident occurred one day while I was standing in the backyard of our home in Chilesburg. I was in elementary school at the time. We must have been about 40 yards from the road, when a group of White children who lived about a mile and a half down the road from us was walking on the road in front of our house. For some reason, they decided to yell at us and call us "niggers." Again, Mama would say, "Don't say anything." And we didn't. The thing that puzzled me most was that our home was nicer and cleaner than their home; I had heard that they had chickens in their basement. How could they think they were better than us? In our neighborhood, however, every family knew the other families, White or Black. So, our complexion was not a factor in this situation.

After we closed the restaurant permanently, Mom took a job in Glen Allen, Virginia, not far from Richmond, which was a long drive from our home through crooked roads. She worked at a chicken plant/factory, along with Aunt Lillian. Dad continued to work at the plant in Fredericksburg, Virginia.

As a young child, I had not paid attention to the bus that picked my father up for work at the Sylvania Plant. But one night when I was in high school, I was practicing my clarinet in the dining room and was up late enough to see him get on the bus. Both of my uncles who lived in homes on either side of us also worked at the Sylvania Plant and also rode this same bus. The interior lights were very bright, so I could easily see Dad boarding it. When Dad got on the bus, he walked to the back of the bus although there were only a few White men seated on it and other seats were available in the front. This was the indignation he had to deal with as a Black man on a daily basis. His hair was thick but he was about the same complexion as the others, yet he knew his place.

While in seventh grade, I turned 13 that February. I had never had a birthday party before, so Mama decided to give me one on this birthday. But as my mom was coming home that evening from work, she had an accident. At the time my dad owned a blue pickup truck. Pickup trucks were not as popular then; they were acquired not only for transportation but also for jobs needed in maintaining our home or hauling. They were more utility vehicles than the "thing to have" because everyone else was driving them. My birthday cake had been placed in the uncovered cargo bed of the truck as Mom and Aunt Lillian rode up front. I was told that while Mom was maneuvering to try to avoid an accident, Aunt Lillian panicked, grabbed the wheel and made it worse, which resulted in flipping the truck over. Of course, my cake did not survive the accident very well. There was gravel all over the top of it. I don't remember anything else that happened at my birthday party. Fortunately, neither my mom nor Aunt Lillian was injured.

I don't recall any other major event occurring during this year except that I began my menstrual cycle a couple weeks before my 13th birthday. Talking about this was taboo in our family. My mother never told me anything about this change that had taken place in my body. The only thing that was said related to sex was "You don't want to be like...who got pregnant." I didn't know how she got pregnant or anything about the changes that occurred during puberty. Just to show how naïve I was, one day we had a dance at our high school during the school day. Later that month my period was late, and I thought that because I had slow dragged and danced real close with a boy, I was pregnant.

When my first period started, I didn't tell my mother. I told my sister, who was about three and a half years older than I, and she told me what to do. Back in those days, Kotex (sanitary napkins) had been invented, but it wasn't unusual to use a rag and wash it if you didn't have sanitary napkins available. And that was what I had to do on my first day. I guess that is how the expression, "She's on the rag" came about. My mother didn't waste any time going to school and telling Miss Upton. So as a result, Miss Upton kept all of the seventh-grade girls in at lunchtime and talked about the menstrual cycle and related hygiene. My mother also told all of my aunts, four of whom lived in the neighborhood. I was so embarrassed.

Aunt Eunice

Aunt Eunice was married to my father's brother, Eddie. They did not have any biological children. Uncle Eddie, along with two of his brothers, had served in World War II. I was told that Aunt Eunice and Uncle Eddie met in New Rochelle, New York, where he was employed as a butler/chauffeur for Norman Rockwell and the owner of the A&P grocery chain, and she was employed as a maid. However, she said she was a governess. Since Uncle Eddie was stationed in France during World War II, he had learned a few phrases in French and would use them on occasion. But one of his favorite sayings was an English one, "You're looking good." He was very thin and liked spicy foods. Everyone loved him. Uncle Eddie had a glass eye. I always thought it was from an injury he suffered during the war, but I later found out that he was badly beaten and robbed in Harlem, New York. He almost died. Their home was to the left of ours with the Baber family's cemetery between our homes. Because the Baber family's home was located over a mile west of us, I never understood why it was situated there.

Aunt Eunice was also known for having dyed red hair—I think what she used was called "henna." Quite a few small moles were scattered all over her face. When she would show off or wanted to attract attention, she would throw up her skirt/dress, exposing her red drawers (panties). I don't think many country women wore red drawers. She was always noticeable because of her loud voice and flamboyant attire. Because she had games, puzzles, and always made the best chocolate fudge with walnuts, all of the children in the neighborhood liked to visit her. Nevertheless, just because she provided these things didn't mean she was the kindest person to children. I can tell you some horror stories, and I will begin now.

There was a girl named Anna who was placed in foster care with Aunt Eunice. I often played with her, and we would visit back and forth from house to house because we lived next door to each other. One day Anna came over to our home about the time we were eating dinner and my mother offered her dinner; she said, "No thank you, I'm not hungry." We noticed that she had on gloves. When we inquired about them, she didn't respond. My mom took the gloves off and discovered that her hands had blisters on them as if they had been burned. We believed that Aunt Eunice had held her hands down on the stove to punish her. I had witnessed her kick Anna down the steps of the front stoop of her house. Once she ran away from home and ended up under the same apple tree as me, the one time I ran away. A few years later Anna left Aunt Eunice's, and we never saw her again. I always wondered what happened to her, but I knew that she had to be in a better place.

Another time, a young girl who lived not too far from us had given birth to a baby out of wedlock and Aunt Eunice

Anna and me

was asked to keep the baby. She became a foster parent to this child. During this time, cotton diapers were washed and reused on babies as disposable diapers had not been developed. If they had, we didn't know about it. I remember on one occasion when Aunt Eunice was changing her diaper, because she was crying (as babies usually do) and wouldn't keep still, Aunt Eunice took the safety pin she was using to fasten the diaper and stuck her with it. I am sure she suffered many more abuses that I never saw during her childhood there.

As for me, there were many instances when Aunt Eunice made me feel bad. One time as a Christmas present, I remember her giving my sister, Lucille, a beautiful doll and a pair of gloves; I received a roll of one hundred pennies. I was young, but I guess she also thought I would think that a roll of one hundred pennies was worth more than what she had given my sister. My sister was also her favorite. On another occasion, my mother had given me a watch for Christmas; I think I was about 12 years old. I spent a night over at Aunt Eunice's and slept on the couch in the living room, where I placed my watch on the end table next to the couch. The next morning when I woke up, I discovered that the watch had disappeared. Because I had heard that she had taken things from other people, I began searching around her house for it. I found my watch in the top drawer of the buffet in the dining room. But I had been taught not to steal and I knew it was wrong for me to be searching through her house, so I was afraid to take my watch back. I felt she would know that I took it and punish me. Really stupid of me, wasn't it? I never saw my watch again. She had done a similar thing after I had returned home from a visit with my aunt in Washington. While visiting her, red ants from her home had invaded my suitcase and clothes. My mom suggested that I leave my clothes in the suitcase out in our garage for a while to allow them to vacate. Everything disappeared, including the suitcase. We assumed that Aunt Eunice was the culprit. Of course, when a person steals, no one usually sees him/her, so we had no proof.

Another incident involved a girl who was in foster care with Cousin Carrie. She was dark-skinned and had very short, curly hair. We played together, attended school together, and eventually became friends. Aunt Eunice, who was light-brown-skinned and also had curly hair, told her that I didn't want to play with her because she was too Black. This caused a strained relationship between me and my friend for a while. But eventually, after my friend discovered the way she treated people, she told me what Aunt Eunice had said about me. In spite of this incident, we were able to maintain our friendship. Aunt Eunice would actually talk about my mother. Except for calling my mom by name, she would say she didn't understand why older women would wear ponytails. At that time my mother was in her thirties; I think Aunt Eunice was jealous because of the type of hair my mom had.

Aunt Eunice had a dog named "Lucky." He was black but I don't know the exact breed. When I was about five years old, one day while my brother and sister were at school, I decided to visit her. She told me not to pet her dog. As I was

Aunt Eunice's dog, Lucky. I am to the left.

sitting on the woodpile behind her house, Lucky came and sat beside me; I guess I was fooled by his demeanor, so I began to stroke/rub his back. But within a split-second, he jumped and bit me on my lip. The bite was painful and drew blood; I cried for a long time. Aunt Eunice rushed out of her house and administered first aid; she cleaned me up and put me in the baby bed she had in her house, where I fell asleep. After I woke up, I returned home. But when Daddy got home from work and found out that I had been bitten, he grabbed his rifle and headed over to Aunt Eunice's to find Lucky. Lucky for Lucky, he had run away from home! Because Dad didn't find him at that time, he lived to see another day. Otherwise, he might have been a dead dog!

On Saturday nights my sister, brother, and I would occasionally go over to Aunt Eunice's and watch a late show called *The Thriller*, that featured the old, original movies such as *Dracula*, *The Mummy*, *Frankenstein*, and *The Werewolf*. I think Boris Karloff was the host. As we watched the movies, she would give us a big bowl of ice cream. While we were shivering watching the scary movies, the ice cream made us shiver even more. But for some strange reason, we enjoyed this. It was usually late at night and in the country, there were no street lights. Years later we would have tall poles in our backyards with floodlights, but during this time it was "pitch black." Our home wasn't far away, but we had to pass the Baber's cemetery in order to get there. The cemetery had a barbed wired fence around it; weeds covered the lower part of the fence, but wild grapes would grow on the back of the fence in the summertime. Rectangular in shape (about

20 yards wide and 40 yards long), with tombstones scattered throughout the entire space, it always seemed colder when we passed that cemetery; we would try not to look at it. There was also a path in the back of the cemetery that connected our home to Aunt Eunice's, but at night we would always take the road. Getting a running start, we would jump over the ditch and hit the road running, not stopping until we got home.

Bad News

I remember the phone call that left my mom crying. It was from the Dean of Women at Virginia State College, where my sister was a sophomore. This call caught my attention because it was very unusual for us to receive a long-distance call from the college. But as the conversation progressed, I could tell that the phone call meant bad news. My mom didn't tell me what the conversation was about; she never really repeated the details of it. However, as time passed, I observed what was happening at home and overheard conversations between Mom and Dad that helped me figure out what was going on. My sister was pregnant and could no longer remain at the college. During those days, girls could not be pregnant and remain in college, nor in high school, for that matter.

While at home over the summer after completing her first year of college, my sister had managed to conceal her pregnancy since it was in the early stages. She returned to college for her second year in spite of her condition. As the pregnancy progressed, she strapped down her stomach and wore loose clothes to avoid others noticing. But she was unable to alleviate the morning sickness that resulted in her not attending classes. This was brought to the attention of the Dean of Women. She informed my mother of my sister's condition and told her to come get her.

This was one of the biggest letdowns for my father. His favorite had really messed up. My Aunt Ruth (dad's oldest sister), whose husband was the Business Manager at Virginia State College, said to him, "That's what you get for putting all your eggs in one basket." Lucille was his heart and now she had broken it. Over time I had observed that Dad seemed to favor Lucille. Sometimes he would take her places like Jones Beach in New York and leave me at home. He would always say, "My Deal, My Deal," and many times he compared me to her as far as my reactions or responses to things. "Why can't you be more like your sister?" he would ask. She was more of an extrovert and I was more of an introvert. I remember once when my parents bought a new dining room set. After we arrived home from school that day, Lucille really noticed it and expressed how much she liked it. But I had to be asked about the new dining room set in order to get a response. When I was younger, I realized that my sister was the first child, the oldest and my dad's favorite; my brother was the second child, the first boy and named after my father; and I was the third child, the baby of the family. My mother's name was Fannie Anne and my name is Patricia Anne. Since she gave me her middle name, for a while I thought I was my mom's favorite, until my youngest brother, Ronnie, was born. He became the baby of the family. This made me wonder, how am I special in my family? Being the third child didn't seem to have much significance.

So Mom and Dad went down to Petersburg to get Lucille. To avoid people in the community finding out about her pregnancy, they didn't bring her back home to Chilesburg. It would be months after the baby was born before she would return home, and then there was a very painful ordeal she would have to endure. Because my father was a deacon in the church, I don't know if this was his idea or if it was required by the church, she had to stand in front of the congregation during one Sunday church service, confess her sins, and ask to be taken back into the church. This was very difficult for her. I think it was more for my dad's benefit than my sister's. As I watched her that Sunday, I felt so bad for her. I don't remember any other girl or woman in the church having to do this.

Union High School

In 1959, I began high school. When I was a student at Union High, I did not appreciate all of the hard work and challenges that our ancestors endured in order to provide a high school education for us. Because of the vision and commitment of a small group of Colored men, Colored children were provided the opportunity to have a secondary education. These men were members of the Caroline County Sunday School Union. They purchased property, hired workers to construct the school (some volunteered their time), paid teachers, etc., in order to accomplish this.[7] I have mentioned the "separate but equal law" enforced in the state of Virginia, and that in the early 1900s when the public school system had been established, there was very little financial support for the education of Colored/Negro children. Thus, Ebenezer Elementary (my dad's school), St. John Elementary, Balty Elementary, Union Elementary, Union High, and other Colored schools throughout the county were subsidized or supported by churches. Union High School began as a private school (Bowling Green Industrial) with five students and one teacher.[8] Later, out of financial necessity, it was turned over to the county school board and became Caroline County Training School. But the Sunday School Union still was responsible for most of the funds to support the school. After receiving accreditation, the name was changed in 1929 to Union High School in recognition of the Caroline County Sunday School Union's contribution to its development. At the same time, it had evolved into a four-year accredited public high school. In 1947, when Virginia adopted the 12-year high school system, Union High did also.[9]

Because there was only one high school for Black students in the county, one way or another, every Black family knew someone in the other families. Likewise, every teacher knew every family in the county since many of them had taught two or more generations of them. As a matter of fact, my Home Economics teacher (I don't think they offer this subject in high schools anymore) taught my sister and my mother. Being the third child in my immediate family to attend this high school, I don't know if I was trying to prove anything, but I worked very hard to get good grades; I graduated salutatorian of my class. My brother and sister had some of the same teachers, but academically, they did not excel as well as me. Nevertheless, the teachers always compared us to one another. Maybe a different type of psychology was taught during those days.

After being promoted to eighth grade, all of the elementary students attending the various one- and two-room schools in the county were bussed to Union High School, the only high school for Black students. The building was a relatively new, brick building with indoor plumbing and central heat. This, I believe, was an effort to accommodate or appease the Black community as far as the "separate but equal" law.

The high school for the White students was not as nice as ours; it was an older wood-frame building, but for years had indoor plumbing and central heat. Although most of the students that had attended the different elementary schools with me were also at Union High, I don't recall being teased or harassed while in high school. I think because there was such a diversity of students, with the different complexions of our race, everyone was accepted. High school consisted of eighth through twelfth grades. Therefore, we were also more mature at this age.

One good thing that happened when I began high school was that my older sister had lost interest in playing the clarinet (bad for her, good for me) and of course, I got the "hand-me-down" when I expressed an interest in playing in the school band. I signed up for band and this was the beginning of a lot of great experiences in my life.

Mrs. Tipton was the band director at our high school, one of the few Black, female directors in the state during that time. And it was through her efforts that our band began to develop and compete on a statewide level. She was very strict and demanding. Marching band rehearsals were held after school and I lived about 20 miles away. The girls' basketball team also practiced after school; I tried out for it and made it but could not be on the team because I did not have any way to get back and forth for practice. My parents did not feel it was important enough for them to pick me up after school. I suppose that their work schedules and the cost of gas were also factors. So I did a lot of things to get home in order to attend band practice.

Sometimes I would spend the night with my maternal grandparents, who lived about two or three miles from the school. Catching rides to their home was sometimes challenging, but easier than catching a ride to my home in Chilesburg. I enjoyed staying with my grandparents even though they didn't have indoor plumbing in the kitchen or indoor bathrooms. The toilet was outside. The "outhouse" was separate from the main house and a distance away; as a result, there were some risks. Aside from not having toilet paper when you might have needed it most, there could be any kind of insect, spider, animal or even a snake lurking inside this place. Once, my maternal grandfather was bitten by a black widow spider while using the toilet, right on his penis, of all places! Fortunately, he was rushed to the hospital and survived. During the night, we had indoor pots or "slop jars" to use and we would empty them in the morning, just like we did at my paternal grandfather's home.

I would sleep on the sofa bed in the dining room where there was a wood stove. I loved to sleep in Grandma's long, flannel nightgowns, which she would give me when I unexpectedly spent the night there after band practice. In the morning I wouldn't get out of bed until Grandpa made the fire and the room was nice and warm. I guess the house was about 80 yards from the road where the school bus stopped. In order to get to the house, we had to first walk through or find a spot to jump over the stream of water that flowed through the ditch and driveway. The water was clear, very shallow, and we played in it; we even caught tadpoles there. Everyone visiting the house, whether in a car or on foot, had to pass through this little creek.

On a few occasions I'd catch a ride with Mr. Beverly—our math teacher, bus driver, and friend of our family. I remember on one occasion a boy who was a student at Union High drove me home. I had the hardest time getting home because he kept trying to force himself on me. I was a virgin and planned on being one for a long time. I felt that I was under a lot of pressure (mostly self-imposed) not to get pregnant, and this continued throughout college. My father had told me that he wasn't going to pay for me to go to college because, his exact words were, "You're gonna end up just like your sister." Nevertheless, I wanted to prove to him that I was capable and worthy of pursuing a college degree. My mother, on the other hand, told me that I was going to college even if she had to work. So she did.

This was the early '60s, and my parents didn't know much about nurturing self-esteem or racial pride. When I was in elementary school and the other children would tease or harass me, I would tell my mom and she would say, "They can't take away what you have in your brain." I interpreted that as meaning if I was smart in school, nothing others would say could change that. I think I had some degree of self-esteem but I didn't think of it as racial; nothing was said to me at home one way or the other. I do remember my mom telling me not to think I was better than anyone else.

It was not until my senior year at Union High (1964), when we had an assembly program that included a guest speaker, a young lady from Fredericksburg, Virginia, that my whole perspective about being Black changed. I remember sitting in the auditorium listening intently; I don't remember her exact words, but there was something she said that really touched me and has remained with me all of my life—a sense of pride and an awareness of our forefathers who had accomplished great things.

Also during my senior year, on November 22, 1963, while sitting in French class, an announcement by the principal was made over the PA system and was heard throughout the school. President John F. Kennedy had been assassinated. Everyone in the class lowered their heads; most were shocked and began to cry. Upon arriving home that evening, the television was on with the newscasters rehashing this tragedy, commenting and speculating about the assassination. My parents, of course, were crushed, as were most Black people in our country because President Kennedy seemed to have been the president who would have been able to make a difference for those of us in our society who were underserved and discriminated against. We witnessed the funeral on TV and admired the strength of his widow, Jackie Kennedy; his son, John, pulling at our heartstrings when he saluted as the coffin of his dad passed. Little did we know that Vice President Lyndon B. Johnson, a White Southerner from Texas who was sworn in as president immediately upon Kennedy's death, would be instrumental in pushing many of the civil rights bills through Congress.

In 1964, my senior year at Union High, we were still in a segregated school even after the *Brown v. Board of Education* ruling in 1954, wherein the Supreme Court declared the "separate but equal" (Jim Crow) or *Plessy v. Ferguson* decision illegal. Even though I attended school during the time of the *Brown v. Board of Education* decision, I don't remember this being discussed with us in school or even at home.

A New Addition to Our Family

In 10th grade, I had to help care for my niece, Debbie, who was just a few months old. After dropping out of college, Lucille was taken by my parents to one of my father's sister's home in Washington, DC, so she could have the baby at a hospital there. Debbie was born in January at Freedman's Hospital, the hospital for Negroes. After leaving the hospital, my sister moved with her new baby to the home of my father's brother (Henry) and his wife in Washington. Once she recovered from childbirth, Lucille started looking for a job in the city, so Mom and Dad told her to bring Debbie to our home in Virginia to stay until she was capable of providing for her baby. Although Mom was supposed to take care of her, I did a lot of the work because my mom also had a job working at the chicken factory.

My mom left for work early in the morning, about 4:30 a.m., and Dad was working shifts at the plant in Fredericksburg and wasn't home in the morning most of the time. Because Debbie's crib was in my mom and dad's bedroom, I would wake up, go downstairs to their bedroom, and sleep there until time to give Debbie her bottle. During those days we prepared formulas that consisted of a mixture of Carnation evaporated milk, water, and Karo syrup. Before giving her the bottle, I would go into the kitchen, take out a saucepan, place some water in it, and heat the bottle with the formula in it. A couple of times I fell asleep while waiting for the bottle to get warm, and all of a sudden, I would hear something explode! When I reached the kitchen, I saw milk dripping from the ceiling. The water had completely boiled away and the glass bottle had burst because the saucepan had become too hot. My luck would be that this was the last of the formula, so I would have to make it all over again from scratch. I also had to clean up the mess the explosion had made, which included sweeping up all the glass, cleaning the stove, washing the ceiling, and scrubbing the floor. What a way to start the day!

Before catching the bus to school, I would carry Debbie next door to Aunt Lillian's house (my mom's sister) to stay during the day. When I came back from school, since my mom was working and wasn't home, I would pick Debbie up. After about 18 months, my sister had found a job working at the Industrial Bank in Washington, DC (Black-owned), thanks to my maternal aunt, Clara Bow, who had been employed there for several years. Lucille had a job with a steady income and was enjoying her life in the city, so Dad told her that it was time to come and get Debbie.

After Debbie left, I still had to deal with my parents' attitudes and the possibility of my getting pregnant. Sometimes, I just wanted to be invisible. I wasn't allowed to date during my high school years. The junior and senior proms were the exceptions. However, I was allowed to have boys visit me at home on Saturdays or Sundays during my senior year. At times, as my boyfriend and I sat on the sofa in the living room, Daddy would make occasional trips through the dining room behind us. If I stepped outside to say goodnight, Mama would flash the porch lights. My parents had not been very lenient on Lucille during her high school years; however, we were living at the grill when she was in high school. This being the case, she had more opportunities to socialize with male and female friends. Sometimes she would take advantage of having older girlfriends and was allowed to hang out with them. But once we returned to our home in Chilesburg, my friends lived a long way from our home, the closest may have been about 12 miles away, so I had less of a social life. Nevertheless, I continued to excel in high school academically, but had also begun participating in band festivals and competitions. My junior year, I won second place in the Omega Talent Hunt Solo and Ensemble Contest, held at Virginia State College. This was a statewide competition. But since the Virginia schools were not totally integrated, only the Black students participated. An article appeared in our local newspaper, *The Caroline Progress*, acknowledging my participation and the prize awarded. I was hoping that these achievements would impress my parents.

A Special Opportunity

During my senior year, Mrs. Tipton, my band instructor who was a graduate of Virginia State College, introduced me to Dr. Gatlin, chairman of the Music Department at Virginia State. Along with being an instructor, he was also conductor of the marching and concert bands. He needed a tenor saxophone player to complete the saxophone section for the concert band's tour in the spring. Since I played clarinet, it was relatively easy for me to transfer to the tenor sax; I had just begun playing tenor sax in the marching band at the beginning of my senior year in high school. The music was very challenging but I was able to master it and later rehearse with the college band a couple of times before the tour began.

However, just before the time arrived to go on tour, my father had another heart attack, which made my prospects of participating uncertain. Over the years, beginning when I was in elementary school, he had been hospitalized many times because of problems related to his heart condition. I knew when I told my parents that I wanted to major in music they did not consider it a worthwhile pursuit. Maybe if I had said I wanted to be a teacher of any other subject, it would have been more palatable. So I felt Dad's heart condition may have been a good excuse for my parents not allowing me to go on tour with the college band. Although he was still in the hospital, when the time finally arrived, I packed my suitcase and Mom drove me down to the highway, Route 1, at Carmel Church, Virginia, where I boarded the college tour bus. From that point on, I was ready to begin an exciting adventure.

The longest distances that I had ever traveled from home had been to Washington, DC; Sandy Point, Maryland; and Petersburg, Virginia. We performed concerts in several states for one week (Virginia, Maryland, Delaware, Pennsylvania, New Jersey, Connecticut, and Massachusetts). Arrangements for our overnight stays in the different locations where we performed were made by the local alumni chapters. In some cases, these were homes of alumni while others were just members of the community who volunteered to provide housing. I especially remember a family that I stayed with in Waterbury, Connecticut. They were White and lived in a beautiful home on a hill overlooking a panoramic view of the city. At night, the city lights were so beautiful. Being from the segregated South, I had never experienced anything like this before. This was my first close encounter with the White race. The night spent with this family turned out to be a very positive and rewarding experience.

As the end of our senior year approached, we all prepared for the Junior-Senior Prom, which was held in the school gym. It was decorated based on a theme the junior class had chosen and we always had live music. The boys wore tuxedos and most of the girls wore formal evening gowns. This was also a special time because my parents were hosting an after-prom breakfast. Our home was large enough to accommodate a large number of students, so a few of my friends and I decided to have invitations printed for the students we wanted to attend. The den, dining room, and living room had tables and chairs arranged so that everyone could be seated. Some of the parents helped with the preparation and serving of the food. After the meal, the tables and chairs were removed and we danced to our favorite songs of the '60s. I have forgotten some details of this event, but my high school and college classmate, Gladys, reminded me that even though we may have stayed up until the wee hours of the morning, we were required to return to school the next day (Friday) to practice for the baccalaureate service. Our principal told us that if we were absent from school, we would not be able to participate in baccalaureate or the graduation program, so we all showed up the next day.

It was a tradition that the valedictorian and salutatorian give speeches at the graduation ceremony. Since I was the salutatorian of my class, I had to prepare a speech. This was challenging because I had never done this before and was unsure if I could do it effectively. Fortunately, I was able to spend a few days with Bill Blake in Washington, DC. He was married to my cousin and was an economist who was very knowledgeable about the topic I was assigned. As nervous as I was that day, my speech was a success.

Transitioning to College

Graduation had passed and I would be attending Virginia State College (VSC) in the fall, so Mrs. Tipton, my high school band director, was instrumental in my being accepted into the college's High School Summer Music Institute. She was a graduate of Virginia State and had maintained a very close relationship with one of her former teachers, Dr. F. Nathaniel Gatlin. Mrs. Tipton and Dr. Gatlin encouraged me to major in music and, of course, wanted me to attend Virginia State. They both felt that the Summer Music Institute would be beneficial in preparing me for my first year of college. My parents were comfortable with this because along with my sister attending Virginia State, my father's sister was married to Virginia State's Business Manager and a few of our relatives had also graduated from Virginia State.

Because my parents could not afford to pay all of the fees associated with the Summer Music Institute, arrangements were made for me to live with Dr. Gatlin and his family. The other participants lived in the dormitories on campus. Dr. Gatlin's wife was a schoolteacher and played violin in the community orchestra. They had a son who was married and lived in Maryland with his family. Their daughter, who was about three years older than I, lived with them and was a student at VSC. She was also a majorette in the college marching band. The Music Institute provided some foundation in music theory and piano, which were requirements for music majors. There was very little exposure to music theory during band practice in high school, and my attempts to take piano lessons in elementary school were not very successful. While attending the Music Institute, I studied clarinet privately for the first time. Dr. Gatlin was my clarinet instructor and he made sure that I got the best piano teacher available, his accompanist. That summer (1964) we traveled to the New York World's Fair for one of our field trips. I had never been to that city and of course, all of the exhibits and pavilions representing the different countries around the world were very educational. Later, while still a student in college, I performed with the concert band at the 1967 World's Fair in Montreal, Canada. Also, while I was in college and during the time when the entire halftime shows for professional football games were televised, the marching band performed for the New York Giants, the Philadelphia Eagles, and the Washington Redskins.

Piano lessons were not so easy for me at this late age. I had attempted to take lessons when I was in the fifth grade at Union Elementary School. I really wanted to take lessons. Mrs. Wilson was the high school general music teacher and choir director who also taught piano during lunchtime. It was just a short walk across campus from Union Elementary to Union High School, so I signed up for lessons. What was most challenging was asking my father for 50 cents each time I had a lesson, so it didn't take long for me to become frustrated and lose interest in piano, not because of the teacher but because my father would always say he didn't have the money. I regret to this day that I didn't persevere.

But my piano teacher during the Summer Music Institute and throughout college was very good. Along with scales and arpeggios, he would also include easy songs. My first piano books were *First Lessons in Bach* and *Scenes from Childhood* by Schumann, which made it more interesting, yet still challenging.

Because I was in the marching band, college for me began in August. Part of my curriculum included private clarinet lessons and piano lessons, and with those came mandatory recitals. Every time I had to perform, my hands and knees would shake. Many times before I would go on stage, I would get an upset stomach. Performing was not what I was about; although I was very good when performing on the clarinet, I really wanted to become a teacher. I successfully passed the piano requirements in the allotted time. Playing in the band was more enjoyable for me. During the first semester, there were always football games on weekends. Since I played in the marching band, I had to remain on campus, only going home during Thanksgiving and winter break.

College Life

Instrumental Music Education was my major in college. It is listed as Public School Music Education on my transcript, but the curriculum for vocal and instrumental music majors was a little different. Mrs. Tipton was a great role model and had impressed me so much that I wanted to teach and share with others the joy and opportunities that music had afforded me. Band tours exposed me to many interesting places and experiences. We also toured the southern states while I was in college (North Carolina, South Carolina, Georgia, and Florida). I participated in different musical ensembles, which included the symphonic band, marching band, woodwind quintet, and jazz ensemble. My performance mediums were the clarinet, alto saxophone, and tenor saxophone. The Jazz Ensemble needed a tenor sax player, so I joined the group. I was the only girl in the Jazz Ensemble with the exception of the singer. During those days, it was rare for girls to perform with this group. Performing on my clarinet, which was my major instrument, provided a means of expression, artistically and emotionally. Sometimes playing the clarinet was a means of releasing stress. There were times when I was homesick, feeling lonely and sad when I was in college, so I would go to the practice room in the music building and play my clarinet for a while, and afterwards I would feel better. Since this was the first time many of the students had been away from home for any length of time, during our freshman year, students were discouraged from going home the first few months of school in order to make the adjustment.

During my junior year, I had an eccentric instructor who taught my Counterpoint and Pedagogy classes. She was a noted composer and had mentored Billy Taylor, the legendary jazz pianist, when he attended Virginia State. Sometimes she would come to class with the same dress on for two or three days. She seemed to have a lisp when she would say, "*Raisth* the windows." When she sat at the piano, she didn't always pull her seat up to the piano; she would pull the piano up to her!

Even with my mom working, my parents still were not able to pay for college. The figure that comes to mind when I recall the total cost of tuition, room and board for the year 1964 is $770. I had a small scholarship from the Alumni Association in my county, but by the second semester, I needed more funds. I had to take out a loan beginning the second semester of my freshman year. In spite of what my dad had said about not sending me to college, he supported me by helping with the financial arrangements. He took me to his bank, Union Bank and Trust Company in Bowling Green, and put our home up as collateral in order for me to get loans until I graduated from college. I was the third child, but I was the first child in my immediate family to graduate from college.

Although my dad never said anything directly to me, he was proud of me. I know this because my aunt told me that he used to brag about me. My parents, like other parents of their generation, seldom told their children that they loved them. Many parents today seem to have to tell their kids every day, sometimes more than once a day, that they love them. We hugged and kissed on occasion, but I cannot recall my mother ever telling me that she loved me or that I was beautiful. This may seem strange to today's society.

I was about 45 years old when my dad told me that he loved me. Maybe he told me when I was a child, but I don't recall him ever saying it. I remember that day; I had driven down to see him years after my mom had died. By this time he had remarried and I had been divorced for years. I had a red Mazda RX-7. As I was getting ready to leave and return to my home in Maryland, he walked me to my car. While we were standing by my car talking, he pretended to check the air in my tires and after he kicked one of them, he told me that he loved me. That was the first and the last time that I remember him saying that he loved me. Parents don't always have to say it. Of course it is reassuring when they do, but you can tell or feel it based on the way they care for or interact with you. For me, actions speak louder than words.

Once a month, especially during my freshman year in college, I would receive a letter and a five-dollar bill in the mail from my mother. That was the only money I would receive to spend as I pleased. This allowed me to go down the hill from my dormitory to a place we called "The Grill" to treat myself to a cheeseburger with lettuce, tomatoes, and mayonnaise, along with French fries and a cherry Coke. I would have enough money left over to buy something else to eat on another day at Foster Hall, located in the Student Union Building. Because I had all of my meals in the college cafeteria and most of the time the food was not as good as my mom's home-cooked meals, needless to say, this was a treat!

During the summer after my first year in college, I lived with my sister in Washington and was able to get a summer job. Fortunately, my sister was willing to help me avoid making the same mistake as she had made and scheduled an appointment for me to see a doctor to get birth control pills. Because she knew I was really serious about my college sweetheart, she thought this was the wisest thing to do.

My first appointment was quite an experience. The doctor's office was in the city (DC) and it was summer. The entrance door to his office was locked when I arrived. Since he was late opening his office after his lunch break, I had to stand outside on the sidewalk in the heat for quite a while. I finally fainted; I fell on the cement sidewalk. By the time he arrived, I had recovered, and after telling him what had happened, I still had to wait my turn. Upon entering the examination room, he made a pass at me. I have forgotten exactly what he said but I know that I felt very uncomfortable.

Once I began taking the pills, I remained on them until I was 40 years old, most of my childbearing years, only taking breaks as required. I was fortunate that I could decide if and when I wanted children. My first husband and I had discussed it occasionally, but each time we thought about it, we decided that we weren't ready. Not having children with him was a wise decision because the marriage lacked the type of commitment I felt was needed for this. I was more interested in having a family where a child could be nurtured by two parents rather than just satisfying a maternal instinct. Much later in life, I decided to permanently take care of my birth control issues. Tubal ligation was my solution. But for some strange reason, as I was being anesthetized and while the doctor was reassuring me of the procedure, I began to cry. I think this was because I knew this was a permanent decision for me and I would no longer have this option in my life. However, I have never regretted not having children; working with children for 33 years as an educator was very rewarding and satisfying for me.

While in college I also pledged a Greek sorority. This would have not been possible had it not been for my paternal great-aunt. When I told my mom I wanted to pledge, she took me to Fredericksburg, Virginia, to visit my great-aunt and told her my situation, so my great-aunt volunteered to sponsor me during my pledge period.

My great-aunt Ida was in her eighties with one long, gray braid hanging down her back. She had a housekeeper and seldom came downstairs; during our visit with her we sat upstairs the entire time. A refrigerator and most things she needed were on the upstairs level of her house. I didn't know anyone in our family who had a housekeeper. She was married to a man with the same name as my father, Chester; he worked as a barber in the town and I understand that the majority of his clients were White men. They were a little better off financially than most in our family.

At that time, more than a semester of pledging was required before you could be accepted into the sorority. I persevered and later became president of our chapter. I was also selected as the sweetheart for our brother fraternity for two consecutive years. It just so happened that I was dating one of the fraternity brothers, but I thought I was respected and liked by the other members of that fraternity as well, since I had interacted with most of them on a regular basis. However, while I was pledging the sorority, there was an incident that made me feel that I was targeted, not because of being chosen sweetheart, but because of my complexion. One night during one of our pledge meetings (these meetings were a part of the initiation process), a sorority member who was dark-skinned pinched me over and over again. I flinched but she didn't stop. The other sorority members in the room could not see what was happening because she was behind me next to the wall and of course, she tried to conceal this from them. She said, "Oh, we have a White girl on our line just like they do at West Virginia State." As far as I knew, our sorority had not been integrated, but she probably had found an article either in the newspaper or in one of our sorority magazines about a White girl joining a chapter of our sorority at West Virginia State College. It was a predominantly black college at that time. When I returned to my dormitory room that night, I was in pain, and when I undressed, I found large bruises on my thighs and buttock.

While in college, I was able to accomplish quite a few

notable things based on my hard work. I made the Dean's List (honor roll) every semester beginning the second semester of my freshman year. I represented my private clarinet teacher's studio for performances on the clarinet and received the Anna Laura Lindsey Merit Scholarship Award from the Music Department (this was awarded annually to only one student). I was also a member of Who's Who in American Colleges and Universities, and the Kappa Delta Pi Honorary Society in Education, among other things.

There was a campus-wide competition for the title of "Miss Virginia State." The three finalists included two members of my sorority (one of whom was me) and one from another sorority. Thus, there was a possibility that the vote would be split between the two members of my sorority, resulting in our competitor winning. There were some other things that I believe may have influenced the outcome. The other member of my sorority was from Richmond, Virginia; there were more students attending VSC from that city than from my rural hometown, Chilesburg, or from Caroline County. I was also competing with the Black Power Movement and the natural hairstyles or bushes; I did not physically fit into either category. To that extent, our 1968 yearbook had a section featuring girls with the various Black, natural hairstyles. I wondered if this was a repeat of what I had experienced in elementary school as far as fitting into or being accepted by people who identified more closely with those who had African features. I will admit, however, it's possible that none of these things had anything to do with the outcome. The person who won was very likable, respectable, and intelligent; we played in the band together during our entire time at Virginia State College. I sincerely liked and respected her. She attended high school in Fredericksburg, Virginia. We also had a common thread—Mrs. Tipton, who served as the high school band director for both of us. After Mrs. Tipton left her high school position in Fredericksburg, she took a position as band director at my high school in Bowling Green.

My sophomore year, I participated in the ceremony commissioning my boyfriend, Jeff, to the rank of U.S. Army 2nd Lieutenant because of his participation in the ROTC program on campus. Like me, he was also from Virginia, but lived in the suburbs of Washington, DC.

He was very intelligent. His stature reminded me somewhat of my father's. He was light-brown-skinned, five feet seven inches tall, very muscular, and had a great sense of humor. He always kept me laughing, sometimes even when I didn't want to laugh. After being commissioned and graduating from college, he was assigned to an infantry unit in Fort Benning, Georgia; from there he was deployed to South Korea, where he would remain for a year. This was during the time when many of the men from our college had been deployed to Vietnam and some did not return. I knew a few who were commissioned and within a few months were killed after their deployment. When I visited the Vietnam Memorial in Washington, DC, I found their names in the ledger and was able to locate their names engraved on the wall.

During my time in college, there were many civil rights demonstrations initiated by students, some in the town of

Petersburg, Virginia. I attended an assembly on campus where Stokely Carmichael, one of the more militant civil rights leaders, spoke. My senior year in college, Dr. Martin Luther King, Jr. was assassinated. When this was announced on the television, I was in my room in the senior dormitory. Most of us didn't have TVs in our rooms, but there was one in every dormitory lobby, so the word spread very quickly.

I had just returned from student-teaching in Richmond; Joe Kennedy had been my supervising teacher. He was a graduate of Virginia State, a violinist who became one of the first African Americans in the Richmond Symphony Orchestra, a composer and an arranger. He wrote and arranged for Ahmad Jamal, a noted jazz pianist. While in Richmond, we traveled to three elementary schools and one middle school in the morning, and in the afternoon, we ended up at Maggie Walker High School. This was the school that Arthur Ashe, one of the greatest tennis players of all times, attended. When the riots broke out in many of the cities throughout the United States, riots also occurred in Richmond. My older brother was a DC policeman and was active during the riots and demonstrations in that city. This was a frightening and uncertain time.

All music majors were required to present a recital during their senior year. This was a culminating performance and an opportunity to showcase all of the skills/techniques they had acquired during their private lessons on their major instrument. It was also evaluated by their private instructor. My major instrument was the clarinet, so I had to select five or six compositions that were of a certain caliber and acceptable to my private instructor, Dr. Gatlin. I also included in my recital a trio for piano, clarinet, and cello. I practiced, alone, for months on these pieces in the practice room until a couple of weeks prior to my performance. Then I began practicing with the piano accompanist. As recital time approached, and I had completely mastered the selections, Dr. Gatlin decided that we needed to rehearse in the auditorium where I would be performing.

So on a snowy winter evening, a week before my recital, he picked me and my accompanist up at our dormitories and drove us to the auditorium in Owens Hall. This was located on campus. As we entered the auditorium, Dr. Gatlin noticed that the baby grand piano was on the floor next to the stage, not on the stage as he preferred. The stage was two steps up from the floor. So he decided to move the piano onto the stage by tilting it sideways with one of the front legs resting on the stage and the other front leg and back leg on the floor. Then, he asked me to hold the piano in place on the stage while he lifted the other side of the piano up to the stage. Even though I was using all of my weight and strength to hold the piano in place, I was unable to maintain that position on stage. As it slipped out of my hands, the piano landed on its side with Dr. Gatlin under it. Nevertheless, we were able to stand the piano upright and he proceeded to coach my performance. We rehearsed all of my selections for the recital, working out passages as needed, paying attention to tempos, dynamics, and other nuances while collaborating with the pianist. After we completed the rehearsal, he drove us back to our dormitories.

The next morning I discovered that Dr. Gatlin was in the hospital. His leg wasn't just bruised as we first thought, it was broken! Usually, students were able to work very closely with their private instructor the days before their recital, but I was unable to do this. Even though he made the decision to move the piano, I felt responsible for his injury. Every day of the week before my recital, I rehearsed my compositions. And each day I would visit Dr. Gatlin in the hospital and we would verbally evaluate my practice session. He would make suggestions for future rehearsals.

The senior recital was a very special event for music majors. Almost everyone in the music department, including professors, attended. In attendance were also friends, family members, and students taking the music appreciation class, who were required to attend and write a critique to be submitted to their instructor. This was the only time, except for graduation, that my mom traveled to Petersburg to see me. (I went home on a few occasions during the school year. Mom and Dad would drive me to college at the beginning of the year and pick me up at the end of the year.) The featured soloist always wore special attire and made sure they presented themselves in a professional way. So I made sure my hair was styled nicely, my makeup was just right, and I wore a full-length, white evening dress with a burgundy waistband. I really felt special and very nervous!

The night of my senior recital, one of the music majors went to the hospital and brought Dr. Gatlin to my performance in a wheelchair. I was truly surprised and happy to see him. I felt great about my performance and felt I had executed it with precision and expression. After my recital, a reception was held in the lobby of the music building.

I had already graduated from college when my boyfriend returned home from Korea. He brought back a wedding ring set; I accepted the engagement ring. In retrospect, I wasn't really ready for this. I accepted the ring because I thought I was in love with him. But while he was in Korea, I dated two other guys and did have some reservations about our relationship. It wasn't long after we were engaged that he was assigned to a base in the States. There had been times that he disappointed me during our courtship. They were very hurtful. One thing I remember, and I don't think I ever forgave him for this, was the comment he made after losing my virginity to him. The pills protected me from getting pregnant, I was in a safe place, and even though the first time was painful, it was not as painful as him saying afterwards that he didn't believe I was a virgin. I had saved myself for this special moment and since he did not actually see the effects of my hymen being torn, he said this to me. Also, when we were in college, there had been times that he had dated other girls while I was on campus studying. During the '60s, girls had more restrictions than guys; freshmen girls had to be in the dorm by eight o'clock at night. While I was on campus, he was off campus having "fun" with other girls; he even had an intimate relationship with a girl who lived off campus while we were dating. However, he convinced me that there was nothing to this relationship and that he loved me. I believed him.

Beginning My Career

In September 1968, I was living with my sister and was beginning my career as an instrumental music teacher in the District of Columbia Public Schools. After being interviewed by three different school systems during my senior year in college, I was offered teaching positions by all. But one principal wanted a military-type person (a man) for the position at his school. In spite of that, the lady who interviewed me was a sorority sister who was willing to present my resume/application to him. I received a token letter offering me the job, followed by a letter telling me that the job had been filled a day or two later, not allowing me time to really respond to the offer. I had had a good experience in Richmond during my student teaching; that being the case, I preferred to work there. But the District of Columbia Public School System extended an offer of an instrumental music teaching position prior to Richmond, and because I had many relatives who lived there, including my sister, I accepted the DC position.

The summer before I began my teaching job, I applied for a summer job in the city. On one occasion, I was interviewed by a White man who was head of the Music Department. I didn't know that he was interviewing me for my permanent job. A few years later, after reading a printout from the school system, I discovered that my race had been mistaken for White and my assignments to different schools in the city may have been based on that. There was another time that something similar to this happened to me at the Motor Vehicle Administration in Maryland when I went there to have my address changed. After I gave my driver's license to the clerk, he stepped away to make the changes, then came back smiling and said, "You want me to change your race too?" I replied, "No, I am Black." This reminded me of a time when I was in high school and my dad was in the hospital in Fredericksburg, VA. There was a drugstore not far from the hospital, so I decided to go there to get something to eat. This drugstore had a lunch counter with stools for sitting and eating in; at the end of the counter was a section for takeout orders. Since I knew I wasn't allowed to dine in, I stood at the end of the counter and ordered my sandwich. About three or four White men seated at the counter looked at me as if to question why I was standing and ordering my food to go. They probably thought that I was White and was in the wrong place.

On another occasion, I was treated by a White dermatologist who received her degree from Howard University. Therefore, I thought she had some exposure to the different hues of my race. However, as I glanced at my file, I noticed she had written White as my race. I felt she should have asked if she was unsure because this may have influenced the type of treatment I might receive since there are skin conditions peculiar to African Americans.

Even in social settings, there have been times, in order for people of my race to feel comfortable around me, that I would have to say something to let them know that I was Black. The women, especially, would be reserved because they thought I was White. I would mention the college I attended, and if the issue of racism came up, I would assert some of my experiences. Sometimes, it seemed as if they thought that I did not have any right to speak on these issues, but I felt that I had been discriminated against more than they, having lived in the South. I felt I had the right to talk about the discrimination that existed in our society because I had experienced these things.

Another time, I was working at a school in a predominantly Black neighborhood where a sixth-grade student, who was Black, approached me in the hallway with a hooked-nose knife. He demanded that I give him the violin I was carrying. I was on my way to a classroom to get one of my students for her lesson. I worked at this school only one day a week, so I didn't know many of the students. He had this knife while he was in his classroom but his teacher either did not see it or did not report it immediately. I told him that since he had that knife, he could have the violin. He laughed and said that he was just joking, but I was shaken. My brother was a policeman in the Youth Division at that time. My first thoughts were to call him and report this; nevertheless, I decided it would be best to follow protocol and report it to the principal of the school.

Sitting in the principal's office, I was still physically shaking when we began to go over the details of the incident.

The principal was the sister-in-law of one of the highest officials in the city and always bragged about how many degrees she and members of her family had. She reacted to this incident by saying, "Because you are White and I am Black, students respond to us differently." I immediately responded, "I am not White and the students I teach have never said anything about race to me." After this meeting I called the head of the music department and she told me that she would speak with the principal. I later found out that the student who approached me with the knife had a record with a long list of offenses, including breaking and entering. Fortunately, every year the school system adjusted the allotments/budgets of each school, they called it equalization, and I was transferred to another school before the semester was over.

Since I was an itinerant elementary instrumental music teacher, I was required to travel to various schools during the week; my first year teaching, I was assigned to four schools. Some years I would have three schools. I would spend the entire day at each assigned school; in a few cases, I would be assigned two days a week at a school. Seldom would I have to travel between two schools during the day. At first, because I didn't have a car, I used public transportation and would have to transfer buses, with instruments in tow. Each school had a different bus route and remembering at what location to transfer buses could be challenging. Not only did I have to travel to different schools, but when necessary, I would have to take a bus across town to carry instruments to the repair shop. Since I was staying with my sister and her family and only having to contribute $50 a month toward food, I used my first paycheck (teachers were paid once a month during those years and my paycheck was about $410 after deductions) to purchase a much-needed car. I bought a new 1969 Camaro for about $2900. My monthly payment with interest was exactly $94.23. Because I was inexperienced and afraid to drive in city traffic, I woke up at four o'clock one Saturday morning to drive my car to Virginia for Dad and Mom to see. Having my own car made a lot of things job-related and otherwise easier for me.

A Night of Terror

After spending the summer and several months of the school year with my sister, her husband, and two children in Washington, DC, I was able to reconnect with a friend that I had known since fourth grade. Our parents had known each other for years. We attended Union Elementary, Union High School, and Virginia State College together. She had an apartment in DC and was interested in having a roommate, so I moved in with her.

Having lived in rural Virginia, where doors and cars were left unlocked during the day and sometimes at night, a certain amount of trust existed among friends and family, with a few exceptions. However, I did not leave the doors unlocked in the city, but I still trusted people. While sharing this apartment, many weekends my roommate went home to see her father in Virginia, and I was left alone in the apartment. One weekend I was invited to a party by a guy whom I had known from college. He was just an acquaintance; there was not any kind of relationship between us. I rode to the party with him but while there, he told me that he had to go to work and that his younger brother, Jason, would drive me back home. Jason was dark-brown skinned, and about five feet six inches tall with a solid build. His hair was probably dark brown but it seemed to be black, thick, and somewhat wavy. I knew Jason and his girlfriend, only to the extent of seeing them on campus and speaking with them a few times, but she was not at the party. All of us attended Virginia State College. At this time, I was engaged to my college sweetheart, who was also a graduate of Virginia State. They knew my fiancé. Because of this association, I assumed there would be a certain degree of respect. I soon found out that I really didn't know the younger brother that well and that he had no respect for me or for himself.

After arriving at my apartment building that night, Jason offered to walk me to my door. When we got to the apartment door, he said he needed to use the bathroom. Being naïve and trusting, I allowed him to come in and pointed him in the direction of the bathroom, which was along the same hallway as the bedroom. This was a one-bedroom apartment; the bedroom was arranged so that after a few steps into the room, the foot of the double bed appeared with nightstands on each side at the head. To the left was the dresser, and on that side of the room was a window with an old-fashioned radiator under it. I don't remember if there was a chest of drawers, but there was a closet on the right side of the bedroom.

While Jason was in the bathroom, I went to the bedroom to throw my coat on the bed, and before I could turn around, he had come out of the bathroom into the bedroom. He forced me backwards down on the bed and began ripping off my clothes.

It was dark and I could see the shadows in the room,

which were created by the street lights. Except for the street lights, there was no other light in the room. I struggled and my blouse was ripped at the shoulder. As I looked around, on the nightstand I saw a knife that I had left earlier from snacking on an apple. Although I was tempted to use it, I was afraid that I would not have enough strength to injure him to the extent that he would not retaliate. I thought that if I failed, Jason might kill me. The telephone was also on the nightstand; it rang and I was able to answer it. His older brother was calling to check on him. For fear of being hurt more, I was too afraid to tell him what was happening. During the attack, at some point, I was able to push Jason off me and run to the entrance door of the apartment. By this time, I was naked. I didn't care if anyone saw me this way; I just wanted to get away. But he blocked me before I could open the door. When he pushed me back into the bedroom, I landed on my knees near the radiator. The window was just above it, so I reached up and opened it. I screamed for help, over and over, to no avail. I felt so helpless. No one knocked on the door to find out what was going on. Again, he dragged me across the floor, pressed me down onto the bed and tried to get on top of me, but I told him I was on my period. Because I had a Tampax inserted, he believed me.

In an effort to get out of this situation, I told him if he came back on Tuesday, I would be off my period then and would be able to have sex with him. So instead of intercourse, he decided that I should masturbate him. After a long time, I complained about being tired, so he began masturbating himself. I had never seen anything like this in my life. When he ejaculated, the semen went up in the air and landed all over the sheets on the bed! After that, he just got up and left.

I was so traumatized that I was trembling all over; I couldn't stop shaking. I was so desperate that I phoned my new friend Reggie, and frantically told him what happened. He came over immediately. I was still trembling uncontrollably, so he held me until I stopped shaking. I had seen Reggie at the teachers' meetings in the school system. But it was not until one night after a session at a music conference, a few weeks before this attack, that we had a chance to talk and spend some time together. After the first time we made love, he said, "I'm going to marry you." Of course, I thought he was just saying that to make me think that he wasn't just interested in me for sex. Also, I was engaged and was committed to someone else. Once I stopped trembling and could speak clearly, I gave him more details about the attack. He suggested that this guy might have been high on marijuana because the way he behaved didn't make any sense. Reggie stayed with me that Saturday night, then my roommate returned on Sunday and I told her what happened. Because my attacker was supposed to return on Tuesday, I told my older brother, who was a DC policeman at the time. I am not positive, but I think the police came to my apartment to examine the scene of the attack. I do remember someone telling me that I should have kept the sheets for evidence, but by that time I had washed them. I wasn't familiar with providing this type of evidence.

When I arrived home from work on Tuesday, sitting at the kitchen table in the apartment were my roommate, Reggie, whom I had only known for a few weeks, and my brother waiting for my attacker to appear. All three of them were there to support me. Not knowing how the confrontation might escalate, I was a nervous wreck. I prayed that Jason wouldn't show up because I really didn't want to put them through this ordeal. We waited for a few hours but he never showed up.

After a few days, I had the courage to tell my sister about the assault. I also reported the incident to the police and was referred to the Sex Squad Division located downtown in DC. As I walked through those cold, marble hallways of the police department, I was apprehensive about discussing what had happened. I sat at the detective's desk and he began to ask questions about the night of the attack. One question, "Did he force you to commit sodomy?" Of course, he had to explain to me what that was, since I was so naïve. My answer was no. I realized that I was lucky in a sense. But he also suggested that this case was not likely to hold up in court since I knew my attacker and allowed him to enter into my apartment. He gave me his phone number and told me to call him if I needed him or if the attacker tried to contact me again. Date rape was not considered a legitimate charge, and back in the sixties, women's rights issues were not the same as they are today. Anyway, I was glad I reported the incident, just in case there were other women he had assaulted or might assault, then there would be a record of this attack. Hopefully, if he was a repeat offender, something would be done to stop him. This was 1969; I am sure today (2020), things would be different.

A few months later, while Reggie and I were in a local store, I saw Jason. I don't believe that he saw me. Although I was nervous and afraid, I did not tell Reggie for fear of him confronting Jason and creating a scene. Years later (about 45 years) at a homecoming football game at our college, as Jason walked past me, he touched my arm to get my attention. I immediately pulled my arm away from him and turned my head. He looked at me as if he didn't understand why I was reacting in this manner. This brief encounter made me uncomfortable, even after all those years.

During the weeks after the attack, Reggie began pursuing me. At first, I resisted because I was engaged to my college sweetheart. But we eventually began dating, and since I knew this was not right and began to have feelings for Reggie, I decided to call my fiancé, who was stationed in the States, to break our engagement. I never told him about the attack.

An Early Death

At the end of October 1970, my mom was diagnosed with lung cancer and died the following January. I remember that day because it was a Saturday, January 15, 1971, Martin Luther King, Jr.'s birthday. I think the DC school system observed his birthday that year, but it would not become a federal holiday until 1986. The disease had totally destroyed one lung and part of the other. Her last days were spent at my sister's home in Washington, DC. Prior to staying at my sister's, once released from the hospital in Richmond, she stayed with Dad at our home in Chilesburg. During that time, I went home after my part-time job on Saturdays and on holidays to help care for her. Eventually, we were unable to find anyone to care for her, so she was moved to my sister's home. By this time, I was 24 years old and had my own apartment. Before I went to work in the morning, I would pick up samples of my mom's blood to be analyzed at Providence Hospital, which was nearby. Her lungs were so badly damaged that tubes were permanently inserted in her nostrils to assist with her breathing. Oxygen tanks were always by her bed. Blood clots restricted her movements, including her arms. That being the case, I would sometimes feed her dinner after leaving work. The day she died, I was working at my part-time job at the DC Youth Orchestra. I began working there in 1969 and over time I held the positions of clarinet specialist, woodwind coach, and conductor for the elementary and junior bands. They called me at work that Saturday and I immediately left and went to my sister's home.

By the time I arrived at my sister's home, the doctor was already there. I went upstairs to the bedroom where my mom was and held her hand so she would know that I was there. She asked me to rub her hands and feet because they were cold. They had begun to turn a purplish blue, and she kept saying that she was cold. She requested morphine, so the doctor wrote a prescription. My older brother rushed to the drugstore to get it. Because my mother's mother died shortly after taking morphine, I suppose she wanted the same thing to happen to her. While my brother was gone, the doctor asked me to warm his stethoscope because it was a very cold January and he had just come in from outside. After doing this, I went back into the bedroom on the second floor and held my mom's hand again. It was the most helpless feeling I had ever had. I thought it would have been better if someone had shot her; at least I could rush her to the hospital and there may have been some hope. But there was nothing I could do; she was dying.

Almost as soon as the doctor injected her with morphine, my mom took a deep breath and gasped. Within moments she was gone. When they told my father, who was downstairs in the living room, that she had passed, he let out a sound that I cannot describe. It was very loud; you could hear the pain and grief in his voice. The night before, he had come up to Washington from Virginia, where he was working. Work for him was a necessity in order to maintain the household and pay the medical expenses incurred during Mom's illness. Mom and Dad spent time together and talked for a while that night before she died. She told him he had done everything he said he would; I never knew what this meant, but they did. In the end, she died of lung cancer at the age of 48. At that time, we had no idea that her condition may have been related to the job she had at the chicken factory; she was not a smoker.

I was engaged to Reggie and was fortunate to have had him to support and console me during this difficult time. On my mom's deathbed, he told her that he would take care of me. After her death, there were times when I would think of her and begin to cry. One day, as I looked out the balcony door of our apartment on the 5th floor, it was snowing and the snow had covered the ground. For some strange reason, I began to cry. I think it reminded me of the very cold day that I watched my mom's casket being lowered into the ground. I thought of all the times she wouldn't be around for me to talk to or to share many of my happy/sad moments with. She died about a month before my 25th birthday and four months before my wedding day. My sister had had an opportunity to share some of her special moments with my mom, but I never would.

On the day my mom died, I remember waiting for the undertaker to come from Virginia to retrieve her body. Almost every Black family in our county patronized

Edwards Funeral Home. Joe Adams, the mortician, was a good-looking Black man. While performing his job as an undertaker, many women admired him and wanted his attention. He was quite a gentleman, gracious and very respectful. He seemed to know how to handle these admirers without making them feel foolish or rejected. To my surprise, my mother's brother, Mutt, accompanied Joe; he lived in Bowling Green and worked with Joe sometimes. We were fortunate that a nurse who was a friend of the family lived across the street, and she helped prepare Mom's body prior to the undertaker's arrival. Joe and Uncle Mutt wrapped her in a sheet, put her on a stretcher, carried her down the steps of my sister's home, and placed her in the hearse.

Uncle Mutt had been an alcoholic since being discharged from the Navy after World War II; one of his deployments included Pearl Harbor. I don't know what his duties were while serving in the Navy. He looked White, but if he was enlisted as Black, he may have been assigned duties such as cooking or cleaning. He seemed to have gotten drunk every weekend, which would lead to cursing and even fights with his wife. When visiting my maternal grandmother, who lived across the driveway from him, I would always try to stay out of his way when he was drinking. Both he and his brother, who was also in the Navy and had contracted malaria while enlisted, returned home from World War II alcoholics. The difference was that Uncle Jack would just drink too much and fall asleep. But in the years following my mom's death, I was told that one Sunday morning, while Uncle Mutt was watching a TV evangelist, something that was said during the sermon changed him completely. Uncle Mutt sobered up; he quit, "cold turkey."

Bobby

After breaking my engagement with my college sweetheart, I continued to live with my friend until shortly before she got married. A few weeks before her wedding, I was able to find my own apartment. Reggie and I continued to date. We fell in love and after one and a half years, we were married. He was a musician and a high school instrumental music teacher. On most weekends, for extra income as well as enjoyment, he would play keyboards in a band. The women loved him and made themselves available to him. This led to a lot of our problems. Nevertheless, we remained married for over 10 years.

As far as his looks, he was light-skinned, about six feet two inches tall, with green/gray eyes. He was adopted and an only child. His adoption was facilitated by a nurse at the hospital for Black patients in Tennessee. When she discovered he was available for adoption upon birth, she immediately told her brother-in-law and his wife since she knew they wanted a child. They were both Black. But his biological father was a White judge and his biological mother was Black. This was Tennessee during the early 1940s. Needless to say, the biological parents of this baby were not married. His adoptive dad owned a record store.

Sales from that, along with revenue generated by jukeboxes and pool tables located in different businesses in the area, provided a very good income. His adoptive mom was a housewife. They lived in a nice home surrounded by over one hundred acres of land. As a result, Reggie was afforded many opportunities; I would venture to say, he may have been spoiled.

On a day-to-day basis, our relationship was very good. We treated each other with respect (of course, the affairs were the exception) and were not argumentative with each other. Although a relatively quiet, calm, soft-spoken person, he proved to be stubborn on a few occasions. Physical abuse was never an issue; but the affairs, which amounted to emotional abuse, tore our marriage apart. When we were dating, there were times when he had affairs, but I was taught and believed that marriage would change this. Over time, one learns that what an individual does when dating is probably what he/she will do when they marry. I could write another book about this. That being the case, I will only mention a couple of incidents that occurred while I was married to Reggie that I will never forget.

We lived in a two-bedroom, two-bathroom apartment and had not been married two years when Reggie's friend, Bobby, came to live with us for a while. He and his wife were living in Atlanta, Georgia. His wife was a beautiful woman and worked as an airline stewardess. They had all attended college together; Bobby also played timbales/percussion in the band while in college with Reggie. The separation made it necessary for Bobby to find another place to live. Since he wasn't working, many evenings when I would come home from work, he would be there to talk and watch TV with me because Reggie often came home late. I noticed and thought it was a little excessive that during the day, Bobby would go down to the corner store to buy doughnuts and other pastries. But in spite of that, he would still be there to eat dinner with me. The craving for sweets, I thought, was just a symptom resulting from smoking weed. Some nights, as hard as I tried to keep dinner warm for Reggie, it was useless. I would go to bed before he would get home.

One evening, the phone rang and Reggie answered it. He came back into the kitchen with this strange look on his face and I later found out what the problem was. Because Bobby was near, for privacy, Reggie walked me back into the bedroom and told me that someone called and threatened to tell me about the affair he was having with a woman on his job. She was White with blonde hair; I assumed a White man had called because Reggie said he had also received threatening notes on his car with derogatory, racist comments. He admitted that he was having an affair and that she was also married. I began to cry and hyperventilate; I couldn't breathe because of the pain I was feeling. I asked if he wanted a divorce; he said no and that he would end the relationship. In spite of the pain and the crying, after I kept asking questions about the affair, Reggie said, "I said I was sorry, what else do you want me to do?" It was as if saying he was sorry made everything better, and it seemed to me that he didn't really care if I was still hurting or not. I felt that he could have been more reassuring and comforting. He did end that affair, but later there was another.

The next day Bobby told me that he heard me crying and wanted to know why. I talked with Bobby about this and he said that he had told Reggie that he would not be allowed to use him as an excuse or to cover for his indiscretions; Bobby sympathized with me. Weeks passed before I began to feel somewhat normal again. The affairs really had an effect on my self-esteem. The two affairs that I was aware of over time were with White women. During the 1960s and '70s, most of the images in magazines, movies, TV, etc., were those of White women. There were not many role models for black girls/women. Therefore, I was one of those black females who tried to emulate some of these images because the man I had married seemed to prefer that type of woman.

So I would do things to try to look like I thought he wanted me to look and made changes to appeal to him sexually. In an attempt to look like them, I bleached and dyed my hair blonde. This was a time-consuming and painful process; the chemicals were so harsh that sores developed on my scalp. But after a while, I decided that I was just going to be ME! He could love it or leave it.

The reason for Reggie's attraction to the physical attributes of White women, if it was just physical attraction, is not clear to me. In my opinion, what's so unique about my race is that there is such an array of skin tones, hair textures, and physical features. Within my race, one can find someone who looks like another ethnic group or race. When I first moved from rural Virginia to Washington, DC, I was very confused. In the rural part of Virginia where I lived, there were only Black or White people; we seldom saw anyone of another race except when we went to the city. Because many of the White individuals in Washington, DC, and suburban Maryland looked just like some of my relatives who were Black, I had a difficult time believing that some people were White. Having attended all-Black schools from elementary through college, for graduate school, I decided to go to a school that was predominantly White. I felt I needed the exposure.

Even in graduate school, the subject of ethnicity was brought up during a discussion in one of my classes. I think it was related to music of different cultures; however, it was not about race per se. There was a White male student sitting in the chair beside me. While discussing this, he placed his arm beside my arm and asked, "Pat, you are the same color as me, what ethnicity are you, anyway?" Another incident occurred when I was informed of a race-based grant available for graduate students, so I decided to apply. I don't remember the title of the grant or if it was for minority students or African American students, but I knew that I met the requirements. To expedite the process, I decided to go to the grant office to get an application. Upon arrival, I was greeted by a Black gentleman who I assumed was in charge of the administering the grant. He inquired about the reason for my visit. When I told him I was there for the application, he hesitated and questioned whether I was Black. After I convinced him that I was, he gave me the application. Nevertheless, I was fortunate that I was awarded the grant which helped cover some of my tuition.

Bobby continued living with us. And then, one morning

when I was getting ready for work, Bobby told me that he wasn't feeling well and was waiting for a friend to come over to take him to the hospital. His friend never came, so I offered to drive him there. I had noticed that the drippings on the commode in the bathroom that he used were very yellow, almost a brownish yellow, but I didn't know why. I dropped him off at the hospital on my way to work; I didn't go in with him because he seemed capable of walking by himself. Outwardly, he didn't appear to be that sick. His wife and parents were notified and they visited him at the hospital. Reggie and I also visited him. But when I asked him about his prognosis, he told me that his liver was bad. His skin was jaundiced and he was very weak. To avoid exposing his true condition, he said he had alcohol poisoning as a result of having consumed a lot of alcohol and not eating properly. His condition was deteriorating.

As a result, Reggie and I had to get hepatitis shots just in case we had been infected. When I went to get my shot, I also inquired about a test for sickle cell anemia. The doctor told me that I didn't need to take the test and I insisted that I did. The doctor lived in the same apartment building as Reggie and me, so he had seen me in the lobby of our apartment building on numerous occasions prior to my coming to his office. Finally, he asked if I had African blood in me and I responded yes. Because my father had been hospitalized a few months after my mom's death and I was told that his illness was related to the fact that he was a carrier of the disease, I wanted to know if I had it or was a carrier. The results were negative. Now I am not sure if Daddy really had it; I just think that at the time they didn't want to give me details about his illness. During his time in the hospital, Reggie and I were married. Because my mother had died four months earlier, neither of my parents was present at my wedding.

While Bobby was in the hospital, I went into his bedroom at our apartment to clean. While there, I noticed a duffle bag on the floor that was open. Being curious, I looked in and found a nude picture of his wife, a rubber cord, and a syringe. I questioned Reggie about the possibility of Bobby being on drugs, but he just brushed it off. Smoking marijuana was something that I suspected they engaged in together but they never did this around me.

It wasn't long before Bobby's condition took a turn for the worse. In just a few weeks, he died. I took him to the hospital and he never left. So my next chore was to clean out the bedroom and pack his clothes for his parents to retrieve. While there I found in the pocket of one of his suits, several little plastic containers with a white, powdery substance inside. After showing them to Reggie, he finally admitted that it was heroin. I asked him why he would put me in a situation like this. I didn't get an answer. To spare Bobby's parents the pain or embarrassment of finding this, I disposed of the bags.

Bobby was Reggie's friend and they had known each other since college and played together in a band. Maybe the reason he returned to the DC area from Atlanta was that most of his friends were there and the drug dealers were more accessible. I don't really know. But this was a horrible experience since he had spent time with us and I had grown to like him. Other than my mother, no one that I had been close to or spent time with during my adult life had ever died. We did not go to Bobby's funeral; his body was returned to Atlanta, where his parents lived. I am almost positive that his wife and his parents knew about his addiction and had given up on him, therefore making it necessary for him to live with a friend.

Reflections

Years passed; Reggie and I divorced. While I remained single for over 30 years, I did the things I assume most single women do and developed as an individual. The experiences I have had during this journey have made me a better person. I accomplished what I set out to do when I decided to teach music, and that was to share with others, students in particular, not just the academic part of music but also the joy and enrichment it can bring into one's life. At an early age, I enjoyed drawing. After my divorce, I pursued this, and along with the poems that I had written, I self-published a book of poems and included my paintings in this collection.

Needless to say, I have no control over my ancestry. However, I am physically a reflection of it. Those experiences during my elementary school years did not leave me bitter. I know that within my race, it was a "double-edged sword." Just as I was teased because I looked White, some of the other children were being teased because they were dark-skinned. Discrimination exists in many forms and for different reasons, not just because of one's color. This is my story about my challenges, but there are so many others, even more horrible, when pertaining to Jim Crow and discrimination in this country.

During the 1950s and '60s when I attended elementary and secondary schools, segregation still existed in our county. Efforts were made by our teachers to motivate us so we would succeed. We learned that we had to work extra hard and be exceptional, maybe twice as qualified, in order to get a job when competing with our White counterparts. Our facilities and supplies may have been insufficient but most of the teachers were dedicated and worked hard and wanted us to be successful.

Although my great-grandmother, Hawzie Coleman, lived with John Karr Sizer and had 10 children with him, I wonder if she had a choice. Nevertheless, I had my own prejudices to come to grips with. One of these was relating to men of different races. For years, because of the way the women of my race were treated during slavery (raped and abused by White men), I had reservations about having relationships with White men, in particular. My pride wouldn't allow me to become intimate with them. Over time, however, after many years of interacting and socializing with people of different genders, races, ethnicities, religions, and political beliefs, I have learned to accept and respond to everyone based on the way they present themselves and how they relate to me, not based on my preconceived ideas.

As a young child, I felt that my parents, my dad in particular, did not give me the amount of attention that I thought I deserved. But there were some advantages of being the third child. Because of this birth order, I had the opportunity to observe my older siblings and learn from them. By the time I was born, my parents were familiar with the different aspects of raising children and were more prepared. My sister was the first child. Much is expected of the first child and the oldest, especially when it comes to setting examples for the younger siblings. My brother, the second child and the first boy, had the family name to carry on. Maybe there wasn't as much pressure on me as I imagined.

Our family was well known throughout the county and had a good reputation. There were skeletons in the closets of some of my relatives that were not exposed until I was an adult, and there are probably others even today. So what if my generation made the same mistakes? Life goes on. Parents, with rare exceptions, have unconditional love for their children in spite of the mistakes they make. It is possible that no matter what I did, my parents would have still loved me. I never doubted that they loved me.

When I was younger, I didn't envy my older sister, Lucille, because of the way my dad favored her. I didn't resent their relationship and I didn't blame her, but I noticed it. I just wanted the same attention that she was getting. When I was older, after Lucille had her baby, I noticed that my mom and Lucille were even closer. I realized that they had a lot to share at that time about motherhood and life in general. As adults, on a few occasions my sister and I talked about things that happened in our family when we were young, including her relationship with our father. We decided that our parents did the best they could, based on their education, financial status, and experiences. But there has never been any animosity between us; my sister has always supported me in all of my endeavors.

As I reflect on my first marriage, I suspect that my ex-husband probably had some issues related to race and family which I, nor he, may not have realized at the time. He accidentally discovered that he was adopted when he was a teenager; his parents didn't tell him. There are many ways in which this may have impacted the choices he made in life.

At the age of 66, I remarried. It was not deliberate on my part, but I married a brown-skinned man and I am helping him raise his two lovely, intelligent, brown-skinned daughters. Although they are not my biological children, fate would have it that things turned out the way I predicted in elementary school. However, I must say that I dated many men of different colors, races, professions, and statuses, but my decision to marry was never about any of these things; it was about love. Hopefully, like Grandpa and Grandma, "Until death do us part."

Acknowledgments

I am grateful to my sister, who provided some details about our family, and to my husband for his patience and support. To my friends and family who took the time to read and comment when I asked, thank you for your feedback and encouragement.

Notes

1. Henry Louis Gates, Jr., *Life Upon These Shores: Looking at African American History*, 1513–2008 (New York, Alfred A. Knopf, 2011), 152 & 156.

2. Maureen Harrison and Steve Gilbert, eds., *Civil Rights Decisions of the United States Supreme Court The Twentieth Century* (San Diego, Excellent Books, 1994),189.

3. Harrison and Gilbert, 189.

4. Maureen Harrison and Steve Gilbert, eds., *Civil Rights Decisions of the United States Supreme Court The Nineteenth Century* (San Diego, Excellent Books, 1994), 165–177.

5. Gates, 255–256.

6. Gates, 229.

7. Marion Woodfork Simmons, *Memories of Union High School: An Oasis in Caroline County, 1903–1969* (Burtonsville, MD, Woodfork Genealogy LLC, 2011), 3.

8. Simmons, 3.

9. Simmons, 6.

Bibliography

Cashin, Sheryll. *Loving: Interracial Intimacy in America and the Threat to White Supremacy.* Boston: Beacon Press, 2017.

Gates, Henry Louis, Jr. *Life Upon These Shores: Looking at African American History*, 1513–2008. New York: Alfred A. Knopf, 2011.

Harrison, Maureen, and Gilbert, Steve, eds. *Civil Rights Decisions of the United States Supreme Court The Nineteenth Century.* San Diego: Excellent Books, 1994.

Harrison, Maureen, and Gilbert, Steve, eds. *Civil Rights Decisions of the United States Supreme Court The Twentieth Century.* San Diego: Excellent Books, 1994.

Peters, Norman to the author, September 20, 1992. *"Grandma was a Dickinson! and Sizers of Caroline County, Virginia."* in the author's possession.

Simmons, Marion Woodfork. *Memories of Union High School: An Oasis in Caroline County, 1903–1969.* Burtonsville, MD: Woodfork Genealogy LLC, 2011.